HOW TO BE A HERO TO YOUR KIDS

HOW TO BE A HERO TO YOUR KIDS

JOSH McDOWELL & DICK DAY

WORD PUBLISHING
Dallas·London·Vancouver·Melbourne

How to Be a Hero to Your Kids
Copyright © 1991 Josh McDowell and Dick Day

Scripture quotations are from the New King James Version (NKJV), copyright © 1979 by Thomas Nelson, Inc., Publishers. The New American Standard Bible (NASB), © the Lockman Foundation 1960, 1962, 1963, 1968, 1971, 1973, 1975, 1977. The Living Bible (TLB), Today's English Version, copyright © the American Bible Society 1966, 1971, 1976. Used by permission. The New International Version of the Bible (NIV), copyright © 1978 by the New York International Bible Society. Used by permission of Zondervan Bible Publishers.

Library of Congress Cataloging-in-Publication Data

McDowell, Josh.
    How to be a hero to your kids / by Josh McDowell and Dick Day.
      p. cm.
    ISBN 0-8499-0881-7
    1. Parenting—United States. 2. Parent and child—United States.
3. Child rearing—United States. I. Day, Dick. II. Title.
HQ755.8.M42 1991
649'.1—dc20   91-1972
                                               CIP

0123459 RRD 987654321

Printed in the United States of America

To my four children. You are a delight to your father, a joy to your mother and a testimony of God's love and grace. Without you, this book would not have been possible.

Josh McDowell

In love and appreciation to:
My teachers and students;
My One Lord—Jesus Christ;
My One wife—Charlotte;
My nine children—
   Five by natural birth
   One by adoption
   Three by marriage
My five, and soon to be six, grandchildren.

Dick Day

Contents

Preface

Despite the fact that Dick Day and I have co-authored this book, you will note that it is written in the first person throughout. We chose to do it this way because so many of our illustrations involve our own families, and it seemed simpler to use first person for purposes of communication. In addition, we often use "he" or "his" in reference to a generic person, rather than "he or she" or "his or her." This is done merely for convenience and is not intended to be offensive in any way.

Dick has taught me most of the concepts expressed in these pages, and chapters 6, 8, and 14 are also under his personal byline. While rearing ten children—six are Dick and Charlotte's and four are Dottie's and mine—we have seen the principles in our Positive Parenting Plan bear fruit in our own families. Now we want to share that plan with you. Dick and I think as one and have but a single goal—to help you become a hero to your kids, and to become better heroes ourselves!

Josh McDowell

Acknowledgments

Every book is a combined project made up of the efforts of many people.

We would like to acknowledge the following people for helping make this book a reality:

To *Dave Bellis* who guided this book project through its many twists and turns and helped shape and mold it into its final form and for producing the video series for which this book is the companion.

To *Joey Paul* of Word Publishing for his encouragement, leadership, and belief in us to publish such a book.

To *Sheri Livingston Neely* for her talented editing of the book and seeing it through its many stages of completion.

To the *"Dads Only" Newsletter* for giving us both insights into parenting that has so positively affected our lives.

And finally, a special thanks to Fritz Ridenour:

> Dear Fritz,
> Thank you so much for using the writing skills God gave you to take our transcripts, interviews, and research and mold them into such a powerful, easy to read book. Your talent with words, spiritual insights, and servant spirit made it a joy to work with you. I trust many kids will be blessed by their heroes as a result of all our combined efforts.
>
> Love,
> Josh & Dick

Part I

Needed:
Heroes with a Plan
for Positive Parenting

AT FIRST the words "hero" and "parent" can sound a little incongruous. Parents have to do so much correcting and disciplining, so much nurturing and nose-wiping that the label "hero" just doesn't seem to fit. This book is built on the premise that parents are the logical ones to be heroes to their kids and offers a practical plan to help them do it. In these first three chapters you will learn:

- a definition for the word "hero" that goes beyond the celebrity image and describes the parent who wants to be a caring role model for his or her children

- why we need heroes in our homes now more than ever

- why millions of families remain trapped in a cycle of dysfunctional co-dependent living from one generation to another

- the most important reason for being a hero to your kids

- how the six A's of positive parenting provide a plan to build a happy, well-functioning family

- why a hero never tries to "kid a kid."

1

You Can Con a Con,
You Can Fool a Fool,
but You Can't Kid a Kid

WHENEVER I speak to groups of parents on "how to be a hero to your kids," I get varied reactions, one of which usually sounds like this:

"Me? A hero to my kids? Their heroes are Madonna or maybe Mel Gibson—film stars and celebrities. Or athletes. My son, for example, likes Michael Jordan in the winter, Jose Conseco in the summer, and Joe Montana in the fall. How can I compete with *that*?"

My answer is always the same. Parents don't have to compete. They don't have to take a back seat to celebrities because, according to my definition of a hero, *parents are heroes already*—all they have to do is start acting like it.

The goal of this book is to share with parents what it means to be a true hero in your home and why it is so important for moms and dads to be heroes to their kids—especially today.

The Family Is under Tremendous Pressure

You don't have to look very far to realize that these are not the best of times to be a parent. The culture in which we have to bring up our children is not "family friendly." All families are under tremendous pressure, and many of them are in deep trouble.

Of the children who were born in the mid-1980s, the estimates are that by the time they reach eighteen years of age, 60 percent of these children will have lived in a home with only one parent present—due to divorce and separation, not death. According to the Census Bureau, one in every four families today has only one parent. Single-parent families are up 150 percent since 1960.[1]

The number of women who have joined the work force passed the 50 percent mark long ago. A report by the National League of Cities says that by 1990, 64 percent of all families in the U.S. had working mothers. In these families were 10.4 million children under the age of six.[2]

Working wives have created a new vocabulary, with terms like "Mommy Track" and "Latch-key Kids." One study done in Los Angeles and San Diego Counties showed that eighth-grade students who took care of themselves for eleven or more hours a week were at twice the risk of substance abuse (alcohol, tobacco, and marijuana) than those who had some kind of parental supervision.[3]

And what do latch-key kids often do while taking care of themselves after school? Undoubtedly, a favorite pastime is television. One source estimates that by the time a child finishes high school, he will have spent eighteen thousand hours watching television, compared to only twelve thousand hours interacting with school curriculum. And while watching television for those eighteen thousand hours, he will have vicariously participated in eighteen thousand killings.[4]

From earliest years, television is as much a part of a child's life as breathing. The average preschooler watches more television in three years than the average college student spends in the classroom in four. One study says that the average five-year-old spends only *twenty-five minutes* a week in close interaction with his father. Yet that same child spends twenty-five *hours* a week watching television.[5]

We Are Failing in Making Human Beings Human

I could go on with reams of statistics that would catalog the pressures on the family that have been mounting for the past several decades. Back in 1970, the White House Conference on Children published its findings in a document called *Report to the President,* which opened by saying that America's families and their children are in trouble so deep and pervasive, it actually threatens the very future of the nation.

The report also charged that, as a nation, we are experiencing a "national neglect of children" by their parents, which has led to a breakdown in the process of making human beings human. If this process is not halted, " . . . it can have only one result: the far more rapid and pervasive growth of alienation, apathy, drugs, delinquency, and violence among the young, and not so young, in all segments of our national life. We face the prospect of a society which resents its own children and fears its youth. . . . What is needed is a change in our patterns of living which will once again bring people back into the lives of children and children back into the lives of people."[6]

The White House Conference on Children released its findings over twenty years ago. But have things gotten any better for the family? From what I can see, the prophesies of the *Report to the President* have come all too true. In the mid-1980s I talked with Dr. Henry Brandt, a well-known Christian psychologist, who told me of his work on the boards of a number of missionary groups who studied applicants for the mission field. He said, "Ten years ago, we saw one out of every three missionary candidates accepted for service. Today, only one out of ten qualifies."

When I asked Henry why there was such a huge increase in the failure of missionary applicants, he said a major reason for many of the rejections is "emotional and interpersonal instability caused by poor family background."

How "Co-dependency" Became Part of Our Vocabulary

Henry Brandt's description of why missionary candidates fail to make the grade brings to mind the new buzz words that are currently making the rounds in many churches: *dysfunctional family, co-dependency, enabling,* and *"toxic" parents.*

According to Drs. Frank Minirth and Paul Meier, founders of the Minirth-Meier Clinic, the term "co-dependency" has been around for several decades and came out of attempts to help alcoholics and their families. The alcoholic was dependent on his alcohol, and the alcoholic's family became dependent on his (or her) alcoholism. The alcoholic's family members may not have been addicted to alcohol, but they were addicted in other ways.

Alcoholics Anonymous used its famous Twelve Steps to achieve considerable success in rescuing alcoholics, but they soon learned that the alcoholic's family would often fall apart just a few months after the alcoholic had dried out. The family had adjusted its lifestyle to accommodate the alcoholic and in many ways had enabled him or her to keep drinking, despite what they felt were honest attempts to stop it. The bottom line: alcoholics are dependent upon alcohol, and their families become co-dependent on alcoholism along with the alcoholic.[7]

Obviously, alcohol or drugs can cause co-dependency, but *any* obsessive compulsion (any thing or behavior carried to excess) can cause it as well. According to Minirth and Meier, co-dependency can also be addiction to people, behaviors, or things as someone tries to control his internal feelings by controlling people, things, or events externally.[8]

The literal meaning of co-dependent is "dependent with." In many cases, a person's co-dependency has been caused by his relationship to his parents and a childhood that left a huge gap in his life.

How many people are affected by co-dependency? Statistics tell us that fifteen million Americans are dependent on alcohol or drugs and that each one of these addicts severely affects at least four other significant people—spouses, children, co-workers. This means that there are sixty million co-dependents who suffer from the effects of the drug and drinking problems of fifteen million others.

Beyond drinking and drugs, we have millions of other Americans battling co-dependency caused by workaholism, rageaholism, sexual addictions, eating disorders, the compulsion to overspend, even an extremely rigid or legalistic approach to living. Minirth and Meier observe: "When roughly one hundred million Americans across two concurrent generations suffer problems of co-dependency, we are embattled by an epidemic of staggering degree. The unhappiness, despair and wasted life lie beyond comprehension."[9]

My ministry to young people and parents leaves me with little doubt that Minirth and Meier are right. Co-dependents are out there by the millions. Many of them are trapped by drugs and alcohol, but many are haunted by voices from their childhood—voices that accusingly say, "Try harder! You never do anything right!"

Others know the recurring feelings of thinking they are not important because parents didn't have time for them. And many more are well acquainted with voices that say, "I'll love you—*if you perform.*"

Minirth and Meier believe the impact of co-dependency is "multi-generational"—that is, the problems of one generation are passed on to the next, a cycle which will continue unless it is broken. Moses spoke of the same problem when he talked about the sins of the fathers becoming a legacy of the children to the third and fourth generation (see Exodus 34:7, Deuteronomy 5:8–10, 6:1–2).

To paraphrase Dorothy Nolte's well-known poem about children learning what they live:

When children live with criticism,
They will learn to criticize and condemn others.
When children live with hostility and anger,
They learn to be angry and how to fight.
When children live with ridicule,
Their self-image shrinks into shyness and false humility.
When children live with shame and embarrassment,
Their self-esteem oozes away into guilt.[10]

I Grew Up Hungry for a Loving Family

Terms like "dysfunctional family" may be fairly new, but I am well-acquainted with the pain that dysfunction can cause. My drunken father was anything but a hero. My mother did her best to love my brother, sister, and me but my parents didn't have a real marriage. They didn't have a relationship. At best, they had an existence. I never once saw my father hug my mother, let alone ever experienced having him hug me. I cannot remember a single time when my father took me somewhere alone and spent time with me.

I grew up on a one-hundred-and-fifty-acre dairy farm just outside a small town in Michigan. Everyone knew everyone else and, of course, everyone knew about my father and his drinking. My teen-age buddies made jokes about him and I laughed at them, too, trying to cover up the hurt and pain.

Sometimes I'd go out to the barn and find my mother lying in the manure behind the cows, beaten so badly she couldn't get up. I hated my father for treating her so cruelly, and to avenge that treatment I would do everything I could to humiliate or punish him. When he would get drunk and threaten to beat my mother, or if he were in a drunken stupor when my friends were planning to come over, I would drag him out to the barn, tie him to a stall, and leave him there to "sleep it off."

As I got older—and bigger and stronger—I did this more and more often. Sometimes I'd be so enraged, I would tie my father's feet with a rope that ended with a noose around his neck. I actually hoped that he would choke himself while trying to get free.

I recall finding my father drunk and flying into such a rage that I tried to sober him up by shoving him fully dressed into a bathtub full of water. In the struggle, I found myself holding my dad's head under water. If someone hadn't stopped me (to this day I'm not sure who it was), I would have probably drowned him.

I grew up not really knowing how to give or receive love. As I went through high school and on to college, I was hungry to experience a family where real love was present. The idea for this book was actually born many years ago, when I saw its concepts lived out in the families of two people who became my lifelong heroes: *Dick Day*, co-author of this book, is, next to my son, Sean, the closest male friend I have ever had. *Dottie McDowell* is the most fantastic wife a man could ever have and a fantastic mom to our four children.

I Became Part of Dick's Family

I met Dick when we were both in seminary during the 1960s. Dick was a few years older than the rest of us, married and with four children. Like me, he was the product of a dysfunctional, alcoholic home. He had come to Christ in his late twenties and felt called to the ministry. We met while registering for seminary classes and hit it off immediately.

I soon became virtually another member of the Day family, often stopping by at interesting hours, like 6:30 A.M. or after 11:00 P.M. to talk about something that couldn't wait. Dick was always patient, kind, loving—all traits that I had known very little about while growing up.

I was impressed immediately by how Dick and Charlotte treated their children and each other. They accepted and appreciated their kids, always encouraging them and making them feel worthwhile and important. And they loved their kids, with affectionate words and touching—lots of hugging. You might say I learned to hug by hanging around the Day family. And they were always available. They always had time for their kids, something that impressed me because my father never had time to spend with me.

Another thing I noticed was that they thanked their kids for what they did around the house. Taking out the garbage, cleaning up—whatever it was—they always made it a point to show their children appreciation for what they did. As I looked back on my own childhood, I remembered that my father had taught me how to work. I could give him that much, but his appreciation of what I did? I couldn't remember much, if any, of that.

I kept hanging around the Day household, drinking it all in, never getting enough because I had seen so little of this kind of love in my own family. In a real sense, Dick's family became the family I had never had.

Dottie's Parents Were Truly Her Heroes

Later, when Dick and I both joined the staff of Campus Crusade for Christ, we went separate directions for awhile. I wound up speaking on college campuses, and it was there I met Dottie. As we began dating, I was intrigued by her constant mention of her family and how much her mom and dad, and brother and sister, meant to her. A few months later, during Christmas vacation, I got the opportunity to meet Dottie's family and, again, I saw those same qualities that were modeled so beautifully by Dick and Charlotte Day.

Dottie had grown up with parents who actually delighted in her. Her mother, especially, was a master at entering her children's world, seeing life through their eyes, and literally jumping into their minds to understand their perspective.

And I was particularly impressed by how much Dottie admired her dad. He was a conventional kind of guy, not flashy, a little straight-laced as a matter of fact, but there was no doubt he was her hero.

As I spent that first Christmas with Dottie and her family, it's hard to say what drew me the most, getting to know Dottie better or getting to know her dad. Right from the start, I began learning from him all kinds of things about what it means to be a loving husband and father. The unconditional love and acceptance were always there. He was always encouraging his kids, affirming them, and showing them he cared.

And just as Dick, Charlotte, and their children had done, Dottie, her parents, and brother and sister all spent time together. They weren't running in every direction, frantically trying to meet individual schedules that were packed with activities. They actually liked being together and they didn't even have to *make* time for it—they just *took* the time because they wanted to.

What's in That Name, "Hero"?

A few years ago, a radio disc jockey polled almost two hundred teen-agers in a shopping mall. Topping their list of heroes was Prince, followed by Madonna and Michael Jackson. Not a single teen-ager named his or her mom or dad. Does that mean that moms and dads are out of the running? Hardly. It simply means that almost two hundred kids equated the word "hero" with their favorite entertainers. But real heroes aren't glittering images on a TV or movie screen; they don't come in for a one-night stand at a rock concert or sports event. True heroes are there for the long haul, and you can see their weaknesses along with their strengths.

For my money, Dick's and Dottie's families come much closer to identifying what a true hero is and does than most of the popular perceptions or misconceptions you will find today. Both of them have always demonstrated to me what it means to be a true hero. Not the plastic, glitzy, celebrity concept often glorified in the media, but solid role models of what it means to be a real husband and father, a real wife and mother.

How do you define that word, "hero"? If you go to the dictionary, one edition will tell you a hero is "noted for feats of courage or nobility of purpose; a hero risks or sacrifices his life." Another definition says a hero is "a person prominent in some event, field or cause because he or she has made a special achievement or contribution."

That second definition ties right in with the whole celebrity craze today and explains why so many parents fear they can never be a hero to their children—they don't have enough "charisma." Dictionary definitions are good for starters, I suppose, but for me they don't quite nail down the real point of what a hero really is.

For someone to be my hero, he or she has to be a person *that I want to be like*. A hero can't be much of a hero if you don't desire to emulate that person, act the way that persons acts, and live the way that person lives.

Heroes Have Certain Things in Common

True heroes share some basic characteristics. They know what they believe and they practice it no matter what the consequences. They're willing to sacrifice their time to make their values come alive. Heroes aren't just talk, their walk bears out who and what they are.

Heroes are never too big to bend down to help others. They never begin to think they are so wise that they don't need teaching themselves. Heroes never confuse strength and gentleness—they can show both when either one is needed. Heroes always share their gifts with others, and they always play by the rules. And heroes never become so used to succeeding that they can't remember what it feels like to fail.[11]

Unfortunately, too many of the heroes or heroines of today lack compassion, ethics, family values, and many of the other traits and characteristics described above. Oh, they may be good at what they do. They may be temporarily popular, they may make a lot of money, but their lives aren't really worth imitating.

A New Definition for "Hero"

In this book, we want parents to know that being a hero to your kids means sharing reality, with no façade, no pretense, no phoniness. We want to redefine the word "hero" as follows:

he·ro (hē´rō) *n*. **any mother or father demonstrating the kind of compassion, character, consistency, and integrity that all add up to being a positive role model**.

Jesus told a parable that has a lot to say about role models— good and bad. He said: "A blind man cannot guide a blind man, can he? Will they not both fall into a pit? A pupil is not above his teacher; but everyone, after he has been fully trained, will be like his teacher" (Luke 6:39–40, NASB).

In Jesus' words lies the real motivation for wanting to be a hero to your kids. It isn't simply because you want to feel important, respected, or loved. It isn't because you want to enjoy warm fuzzies, admiration, and good feelings about being a super dad or mom. Those may all be nice side benefits of being a hero, but they are not the bottom line.

You want to be a hero to your kids in order to equip them to live full and abundant lives in a hurting, hostile, needy world.

Do you want your children to be able to say no to drugs, premarital sex, and all the other pressures placed on them by the media and their peer group? Then start while they are young (or start *now,* no matter what their age) and work at being their hero. The more you become a hero to your kids, the more they will listen to you and live by your values.

How Will Your Kids Turn Out?

Think about it for a minute. Another reason you want to be a hero to your kids is because *they are going to turn out just like you.* Face it, there is a bonding between parent and child unlike any other relationship on earth. To paraphrase Luke 6:40, "Children are not above their parents, but all children, after they are nurtured, will be like their parents."

What do we want to see in our children? Whatever they see in us, we're going to see in them, including their concept of God. In their excellent book *The Parent Factor,* co-authors Robert McGee, Jim Craddock, and Pat Springle state:

> Your view of God, your self-concept, and your ability to relate to others are shaped by your relationship with your parents. If your parents were (and are) loving and supportive, then you probably believe that God is loving and strong. You're probably a secure and confident person, and are able to relate easily to other people. However, if your parents were harsh and demanding, you probably believe that God is also that way, and you may think that you can never do enough to please Him. . . . Whether they have been loving or aloof, kind or harsh, supportive or neglectful, parents have played a major role in forming your view of God, your view of yourself, and your relationships with others. The result can be wonderful or tragic.[12]

We agree! The relationships your children have with you, their parents, will determine the quality of life they will experience as adults. If you are their hero, God will be their Super Hero. They will want to serve Him out of love, not fear—gratitude, not guilt.

If you have small children remember, you are like "God" to them. Anything you tell them, they'll believe. If you tell them the moon is made of cheese, they'll believe you. If your words and actions tell them they are somebody special, loved because of who they are, not how they look or what they do, then as they grow older, they'll resist the temptation to get on the performance treadmill and they'll discover why personal success, status, beauty, and wealth do not bring lasting happiness.

Remember, the world will too soon bring to their young, innocent lives Satan's most sinister lie—you are valuable based *only* on how you measure up to society's standards of success. But if your message is loud enough, when they hear this lie, up from the very core of their being will flood precious memories of love and acceptance to empower them to say "no" to the deception of Satan and "yes" to the sufficiency of Christ.

And to you parents of older kids, remember, it's never too late to start doing what is right.

In this book, a real hero is a mom or dad who lives every day by the principles that Jesus Himself taught. It sounds simple enough, doesn't it? But any parent knows it isn't simple at all. Instead of being in control (the "father or mother knows best" mode), our days often turn into a series of helter-skelter activities to which we react, always seeming to be on the defensive, never quite sure we will ever catch up.

The Six A's Plan for Being a Hero

I know the feeling and so does Dick, but we want to offer some help—a plan we call "The Six A's for Positive Parenting." These six key principles include: *acceptance, appreciation, affection, availability, accountability,* and *authority.*

Chapter 2 will cover an overview of the Six A's plan, and the remainder of this book will develop each of the A's in depth to give you biblical and educational insights, plus many practical suggestions for practicing each principle with your family.

The Six A's plan gives you step-by-step instructions on how to be a hero to your kids. Yes, it's true kids are fascinated and impressed by rock and film stars and other highly visible celebrities. But from what I see as I travel a hundred and fifty thousand miles a year talking to high schoolers and collegians, what they are really looking for is leadership, character, integrity, and above all, love.

The only place they will be able to get the real thing is from Mom and Dad, not Madonna or the "New Kids on the Block." Children know the difference between real interest and feigned concern. They know instinctively how important they are to those around them.

They know when they are really loved, accepted, and appreciated. They know if they are being given self-worth or feelings of worthlessness, whether they're important or insignificant. They can tell when affection comes from the heart, or when it's given out of duty or distraction.

They can't, however, see much difference between "quality time" and "quantity time." It's all the same to them, and when parents aren't available, they aren't fooled.

Never Try to Kid a Kid!

I'm not sure where I picked up the slogan that titles this chapter, but it has become a guiding principle for me with my own family, and I share it everywhere I go:

> **You can con a con,**
> **you can fool a fool,**
> **but you can't kid a kid.**

You'll be seeing these lines again before this book is through. If you get nothing else from these pages, I pray that you understand that your children will not be fooled, patronized, or ignored. Words are not enough. They want to see action.

To be heroes, parents don't have to be perfect. They do, however, need humility, commitment, and a willingness to learn. When children are parented with *acceptance, appreciation, affection, availability, accountability,* and loving *authority,* wonderful things can happen.

> When children live with tolerance and fair treatment,
> They learn to be patient and fair with others.
> When children live with encouragement,
> They learn to be confident and secure.
> When children live with praise and compliments,
> They learn appreciation.
> When children live with fairness,
> They learn the meaning of justice.
> When children live with security,
> They learn to have faith.
> When children live with approval,
> They learn to like themselves.
> When children live with unconditional acceptance,
> They learn to find love in God and the world.[13]

This "Positive Parenting Plan" makes it possible to have all these benefits, and more. This plan is no magic formula. It doesn't guarantee success, but it does provide a compass for steering through all kinds of waters, rough or smooth. Now, let's look at that plan more closely.

To Think About, Discuss, or Try for Yourself

1.   Have you ever thought of why and how your parental role should include the concept of being a hero? Why or why not?

2.   In this chapter Josh redefines the word "hero," putting strong emphasis on the term "role model." What your children see in you, you are going to see in them on down the line. How does this statement affect your thinking about your responsibilities as a parent? What are your children learning as they watch you practice your values (what you say you believe)?

3.   Page 14, contains a quote from authors of another book regarding how a child's view of God, self, and others is shaped by his relationship to his parents. Reread that quote and make it a basis for prayer as you go through the rest of this book.

4.   "Children are not above their parents, but all children, after they are nurtured, will be like their parents." Think for a moment about how your children are becoming like you. Identify two or three positive characteristics in yourself that you would like to pass on to your children and think of ways you can model those characteristics this week.

2

Don't Chance It, Plan It

IT'S OFTEN said that marriage and parenting are two responsibilities that people take on with little or no training. In fact, most of the training they do get is "on the job," with lots of trial and error. It's ironic that so often we seem to leave the most precious relationships in life to chance. We hope that somehow love will conquer all, that "the kids will know that we love them anyway," and "whatever we're doing, it's for their own good."

In reality, we do get very extensive training for marriage and family from our primary teachers, Mom and Dad. The problem is that their role-model instruction is not always according to God's principles.

If what teen-agers across the country are telling me is any indicator, the "parenting by the seat of your pants" approach isn't working too well. Despite an increasing number of books, videos, films, and other "informative" paraphenalia, parenting remains a mystery that many families fail to solve.

Dick Day and I don't claim to know all the answers to dysfunctional families and co-dependency. The plan we are going to describe in this chapter isn't a slick, "can't fail" formula. Nonetheless, we believe that we have discovered some basic principles of parenting that can do much to help dysfunctional families break the negative cycle and help families who are functioning well learn to develop an even more positive, godly approach.

Our goal is to replace toxic parenting with nurturing parenting, and the odds for doing this successfully will be much more in your favor if you use the "Six A's for Positive Parenting." One way to look at the Six A's plan is to see it as a recipe:

You start with *acceptance.*
Then you add *appreciation.*
Season both of these with liberal amounts of *affection* and *availibility.*
Then add *accountability,* topped off with loving *authority.*

Everything we say in the rest of this book will be based on these Six A's for Positive Parenting. Put any one of these Six A's to work in your family and you're bound to build a better relationship with your children. Put all six to use, and you just might become a true hero to your kids!

Be aware, however, that *you must use the Six A's in correct order.* Some well-meaning Christian parents think they should start by establishing their authority. They want to be sure their kids will be held accountable, and, that favorite word, "responsible." Parents concerned with establishing their authority believe that things like acceptance, appreciation, affection, and availability come as a matter of course. As we'll see in chapter 3, it's unwise to take this for granted. Furthermore, working first on your authority is the exact reverse of how to be a positive hero to your kids.

Why Acceptance Must Come First

To use the Six A's plan correctly, you must start with *acceptance,* because it is the absolute foundation of a good relationship with your children. The ideal to aim for is unconditional acceptance—communicating your love in such a way that your children know, no matter what they might do or say, no matter how badly they fail or foul things up, that Mom and Dad love them anyway.

When children sense true acceptance from their parents, they feel *secure.* They know they are valued, that they have worth that is not determined by how well they perform, but only by the fact that they are who they are and that *they are loved for themselves alone.*

Most parents will agree that this is the ideal they aim for, and many believe they are hitting their target. In reality, however, they often offer performance-based (conditional) acceptance to their children.

In other words, as long as little Johnny and Jennifer are "good" (perform correctly), their parents accept them. But if children make mistakes, fail, get bratty or unreasonable, that acceptance disappears, at least temporarily. Parents can withdraw their acceptance very subtly, without even realizing it, but the child senses it in a second.

My own experience with our four children tells me that unconditional acceptance is a full-time job. You don't "vow to be acceptant" and then assume that you are communicating acceptance because you intend to do so. I grab every opportunity I can to let my kids know I accept them, whether they win or lose life's daily challenges and battles. Like me, they are human and they have their good days and days that aren't so good. But my acceptance remains constant.

Accepting Katie, My Soccer Player

My wife, Dottie, and I are constantly looking for ways to demonstrate our unconditional acceptance to our kids. Sometimes I doubt that we are getting through, but then our children come up with observations that show us they are taking it all in. They are listening and watching far more closely than we imagine.

For example, when our daughter Katie was only six, she became quite a soccer star on her own level. After warming up for one of her most important games of the season, she came running off the field and said, "Daddy, if I score a goal, will you give me a dollar?"

"Sure," I answered with a smile.

"Wow!" Katie said. To a six-year-old, a dollar a goal sounds like a multi-year NBA contract.

"Wait a minute," I said, grabbing her before she ran off to join her team. "Even if you don't score a goal, I'll still give you a dollar."

"You will?"

"Yes, I will."

"Wow!" Katie said again as she prepared to scamper off to start the game.

But I grabbed her one more time, saying, "Wait a minute, do you know why?"

My six-year-old stopped and turned around. For at least three years I'd been trying to help her understand what unconditional acceptance is all about, and none of it had seemed to mean very much. But at that moment, she turned, looked at me, and said, "Yeah . . . it doesn't matter if I play soccer or not. You love me anyway!"

My daughter couldn't have said anything at that moment to give me more joy. I don't even remember if Katie scored a goal in that game or not. It didn't matter. What did matter was that she knew I loved her anyway, and that's what it's all about.

Appreciation Says, "You Are Significant"

If acceptance is the foundation of a good relationship with your child, *appreciation* is the cornerstone. Accepting your child builds his or her self-worth and sense of security. Appreciation adds a sense of *significance,* the idea that, "Hey I'm important! Mom and Dad like to have me around—they're proud of me!"

To practice appreciation, become what author Mamie McCullough calls a "good finder." Instead of approaching your parenting task with the goal of correcting, disciplining, and keeping your children in line, put the emphasis in the other direction. Look first for where and when you can sincerely praise, compliment, and encourage your kids.

That doesn't mean you abandon discipline or correction when it's needed. But you pave the way for discipline by letting the child know that you really notice and approve of what he or she does right. Then you can correct mistakes or misbehavior in a positive climate rather than continually feeling, "All I seem to see is what my kids do wrong—I'm always on their case."

Dick and I will have a lot more to say about appreciation in chapters 7 and 8. For now, line it up with acceptance as the two main building blocks that provide the *Love* half of the parenting equation. We will get to the *Limits*—accountability and authority—later. First, we need to take a brief look at two key ways to show your kids you really do accept and appreciate them.

Affection Says, "You Are Lovable"

It seems unnecessary to remind parents to be affectionate toward their children. Unfortunately, many children grow up without it, and the repercussions can be felt many years later. Often, teen-agers who become involved in premarital sex are looking for the love they never got when they were small.

I have always held firmly to the belief that children can't get too much affection. They need to hear and feel affection from you every day. Physically, you should touch them with plenty of hugs, kisses, shoulder pats, and back rubs. Verbally, you should tell them you love them. They can't hear it enough. In person or over the phone, I try to tell each of my children "I love you" in one way or another at least four or five times a day.[1]

It's true that as children get a little older and move into the upper elementary grades and junior high, they may start to act as if they don't need or want a lot of affection. From what I've seen, however, these older children need affection as much as ever, if not even more so. It may be a problem to discover the right time, place, and way to show them affection, but never believe for a minute they don't want it.

Unfortunately, there is a tendency by parents to show *less* affection as a child grows older. One study I've seen reports a definite decline in verbal and physical affection from moms and dads as children grow older. Fifty-four percent of the mothers give daily verbal affirmations like "I love you" to fifth graders, but by the time these children were ninth graders only 36 percent of their mothers were doing so. As for fathers, 44 percent were showing verbal affection to fifth graders, but it dropped to 36 percent by the time they were ninth graders.

As for showing physical affection—hugs, kisses, pats, and so forth—68 percent of the mothers showed it to fifth graders, but it dropped to 44 percent by the time they were ninth graders. Fifty percent of the fathers showed physical affection to fifth graders and it dropped to 26 percent by ninth grade.[2]

No research study can be taken as the "final word," but these statistics clearly suggest that the older children get, the less their parents tell or show them each day that they love them. What do you think it's like for children by the time they hit fifteen, sixteen, and seventeen? It's a good guess that the percentages would have to drop even lower!

It is terribly ironic that when a child reaches adolescence and is grappling with personal identity, trying to build a good self-image and healthy self-esteem, that he or she is quite likely to be receiving very little parental affection.

It won't do to simply say, "The kids know I love them. I don't have to be telling them and showing them all the time." You *do* have to be telling and showing them all the time. Showing affection to children is what gives them a sense of lovability, and feeling lovable gives them the confidence they need to establish healthy relationships with others outside the family. I can't tell you how many teenagers I've talked with—especially teen-age girls—who have gotten into trouble sexually because they were trying to prove that they were lovable.

Availability Says "You Are Important!"

In some ways, availability is the most important of all Six A's for Positive Parenting. Why? Obviously, if you're not around, how will you demonstrate to your children acceptance, appreciation, and affection? How will you help them learn to be accountable and how will you practice loving authority?

In these days when parents try to justify their busy schedules by saying they spend "quality time" with their children, what we must face is that, while quality time is good, there is no substitute for quantity time. Indeed, out of a sizeable quantity of time with your kids will come the quality moments. You just don't sit down with your child and say, "Hi, son, let's spend a quality five minutes together before I dash off to another meeting."

Because I'm so goal-oriented and not content unless I'm engaged in four or five major projects at once, I have had to learn that my kids must come first. In later chapters, I'll be sharing many ideas for things you can do with your kids. Some of them are simple and some of them may seem a bit exotic or even bizarre, but I've done them all and I plan to continue. I want my children to know that I always have time for them—that no person, activity, or thing is more important to me than they and their mother are. And they need to know that my first love, Jesus Christ, is the very foundation of my love for them and their priority in my life.

Love Is Balanced by Limits

Acceptance, appreciation, affection, and availability are all part of the *Love* half of the parenting equation. On the other side, we place two balancing factors: accountability and loving authority, the *Limits* or rules by which the family lives. Keep in mind, however, that *the love must come first*. Love is what makes rules palatable and beneficial.

As we have seen, acceptance gives a child a sense of security. Appreciation gives the child a sense of significance. Accountability gives the child a sense of self-control. As we make our children accountable, they gain knowledge of what it means to be responsible.

Demonstrating and teaching accountability in your family provides a perfect means for being a hero—a good role model—to your kids. Not only does a hero hold his children accountable and responsible for what they do; a hero is willing to make himself accountable to his children!

Dick and I have both made ourselves accountable to our children by asking them to help us be the best parents we can be and by pointing out how we can improve. Our children have the right to tell us, with respect, when we do or say things that contradict what we say we believe or what we're trying to teach in the family.

When you make yourself accountable to your kids, be ready to be held to account! On one occasion, we were all going out to a fast-food restaurant for dinner and everyone except Kelly, our oldest, had the same restaurant in mind. Realizing she was out-voted, Kelly made some critical remarks about the popular choice, punctuated by adjectives like "garbage" and "grease pit."

I corrected Kelly for her choice of language and her less than agreeable attitude, and then we all compromised by agreeing to have those who wanted to go to the first restaurant be dropped off there. Then Dottie and I would take Kelly on to the restaurant she preferred.

We drove over to the restaurant that Sean, Katie, and Heather had chosen and, as we pulled up, I said, half in fun, but half in agreement with Kelly, "Everyone out for the gag bag."

The younger children didn't even hear my remark—they were too excited about the french fries and burgers they were planning to order. But as we pulled away to head down the street to Kelly's choice of restaurant, she said, "Dad, you just did what you told me was wrong—what's the difference between calling a place a garbage can or a gag bag?"

Kelly had me cold, and I knew it. We were headed out for dinner, but I was going to have my own words for hors d'oeuvres. I swallowed hard and thanked Kelly for pointing out my inconsistency and lack of good role modeling. It was a humbling experience, but in some ways, perhaps it was the best lesson I could ever teach about what it means to be accountable and have self-control—especially control of your tongue.

Something Dick and I stress in our parent seminars is that accountability teaches a child obedience, which helps the child develop self-discipline. Without a good sense of accountability, a child will never have the self-discipline to deal with authority.

There Are Two Kinds of Authority

The word "authority" suggests leadership—and that's what parents are, leaders in their homes. When invoking authority, a parent can use several approaches, including the *autocratic* and the *relational*.

The autocratic parent says, "I'm in charge—you'll do it my way or else!" The autocratic or authoritarian parent lives by the letter of the law. Autocratic parents have to control, dominate, and manipulate. Their kids are puppets who react to tugs and jerks on very tight strings.

The relational (authoritative) parent says, "I want what's best for you. Let's look at the options. . . . Here is why I believe this is the best choice—the most responsible way to live."

The relational parent always models the spirit of the law. Relational parents are servant-leaders who authoritatively guide, role model, and set examples. Their children know there are limits, but they also know there is freedom to make good choices within those limits. Loving authority gives a child a sense of self-decisiveness, being able to make the right choice about how to act, what to say, and what to do.

I've already used the analogy of a recipe to describe the Six A's. Another way to see the Plan for Positive Parenting is in the diagram on p. 26, which depicts a healthy, well-functioning home. At the base, or foundation, is *acceptance,* and right on top of that we have *appreciation.* The two "walls" of *affection* and *availability* represent how *acceptance* and *appreciation* are communicated to the child, as well as how the entire super structure of *Love* supports the rafters and roof of the *Limits—accountability* and *authority.*

The Six A's of Positive Parenting are a blueprint for building a healthy, positively functioning family. When you see the Six A's in correct order, you will be a hero to your kids, not for your own satisfaction, but truly for their own good and best interest. You will be the kind of role model they need to be equipped to live in a demanding, even dangerous, world.

But we want to repeat, the Six A's must be used in correct order. You don't build a house by starting with the roof. You don't try to add the foundation later. If you do, you will have nothing but chaos and confusion. In chapter 3 we will look more closely at why *Love* must always come before *Limits.*

The Six A's of Positive Parenting

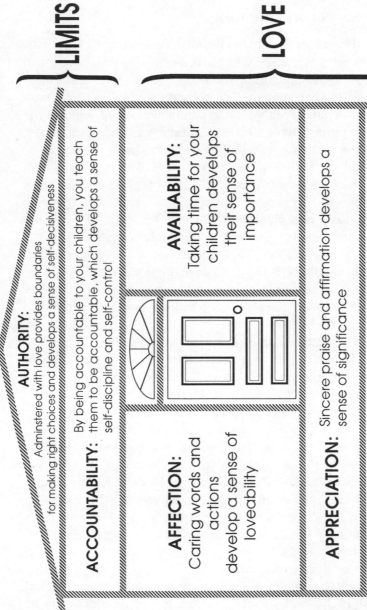

LIMITS

LOVE

AUTHORITY:
Adminstered with love provides boundaries
for making right choices and develops a sense of self-decisiveness

ACCOUNTABILITY:
By being accountable to your children, you teach
them to be accountable, which develops a sense of
self-discipline and self-control

AVAILABILITY:
Taking time for your
children develops
their sense of
importance

AFFECTION:
Caring words and
actions
develop a sense of
loveability

APPRECIATION:
Sincere praise and affirmation develops a
sense of significance

ACCEPTANCE:
Unconditional love develops a sense
of security and self-worth

**Love is the superstructure supporting Limits, the protective
covering of the family**

To Think About, Discuss, or Try for Yourself

1.   How important is it to have a plan for parenting? What has been your plan to this point?

2.   According to the authors, acceptance must come first when parenting your child. Take out a sheet of paper and write down your own statement as to why this is true.

3.   How well do you appreciate your children? Do you find specific ways to praise or encourage them each day? Do your praises outnumber your corrections and criticisms? As your children have grown older, have you slipped into the typical habit of showing them less overt affection? If this is the case, talk with your spouse about how you can be more affectionate in ways that are comfortable for you and acceptable to them.

4.   According to the authors, what is the only way to spend any "quality time" with your children? How much time do you spend where you can focus on each child and give him or her your full attention, interest, and affection? Do you ever plan and then go on dates separately with each child? Is it something that you could begin doing soon? How about this week?

5.   How does the idea of being accountable to your child sound to you? Does this seem to put the parent in a position where the child can show disrespect? Or does this seem to be a good way to model accountability for your children?

6.   According to the authors, two ways of using parental authority that are poles apart are autocratic and permissive. Relational is a balance between the two. Which style would your children say is yours and why?

3

Rules Won't Work without Relationships

RULE NUMBER 1 for parents who want to be heroes to their kids is an apt observation about rules in general:

Rules without Relationships Lead to Rebellion

Children do not respond to rules; they respond to relationships. It's true that you can get your children to "behave" by enforcing the rules. You can control your children to a certain point by running a tight ship, but that doesn't necessarily mean you are getting their loving and obedient response. What you are getting is their reaction, which may look like obedience on the surface, but beneath there is fear, frustration, and anger.

Unless you establish a loving, acceptant relationship with your child, you can almost count on trouble down the line. In fact, Scripture warns parents not to provoke or exasperate their children (see Ephesians 6:4, Colossians 3:32). What these verses are saying is that rules without relationships will almost always exasperate or provoke a child into negative behavior.

28

Dick and I have spoken to parents throughout the nation and around the world for the past fifteen years. Everywhere we go we find families who have rebels on their hands, parents at their wits' end, not knowing what they can do. As we saw in chapter 1, it's easy enough to blame the culture in which we live. There are many likely scapegoats. If only those kids didn't watch so much television, see so many movies, or listen to that rock music.

We're not denying that all of those pressures can do families serious harm. Our children are growing up in a culture that is not dedicated to helping a family; in fact, many of the values of our present-day culture are deadly enemies of family life.

We Can't Blame the Culture for Our Mistakes

It's no wonder that we find so many rebels today—kids who are alienated, angry, cynical, and lonely. But Mom and Dad, please realize that the real problem is not with the culture. We can try to excuse our weaknesses by blaming the culture, but the real cause of the problem lies deeper—right on our doorsteps and in our family rooms.

When parents try to lay down rules without first establishing a real relationship with their children, the natural result will be rebellion. Sometimes it will be outward rebellion that is easy to spot in the child's actions, but just as often it can be an inward rebellion, where the child appears to be obedient but is nursing all kinds of grudges and hangups, along with an unhealthy self-image and poor self-esteem.

We see the "rules without relationships lead to rebellion" principle being violated in every culture around the globe. Recently I spoke in the Philippines to over six hundred pastors and Christian workers. Afterward, over two hundred of these men lined up to talk to me. One of the major problems I dealt with that night is illustrated in the father—a pastor—who told me his family had turned against him. His three children—seventeen, thirteen, and ten years of age— were considered to be "the worst kids in the church" and were all rebelling in one way or another. He wanted to know what he could do.

"Forget the rules," I told him.

"What?" he said in disbelief. "That's what's wrong—they're not obeying any rules. They don't even think they need to."

"I know what you're saying," I told him, "but I repeat, forget emphasizing the rules. Take some of the ideas I talked about tonight and start building a relationship. You don't have anything to lose."

One of the main ideas I had shared with that group of Filipino pastors and Christian workers was to take more time to be with their children. As we will see in later chapters, it does very little good to try to assure your children that you love them or accept them if you aren't available to them. They quickly see through the sham. Never forget: "You can con a con, you can fool a fool, but you can't kid a kid."

"You Never Do Anything with Us!"

A pastor friend of mine learned that principle just in time. I ran into Chris one day and asked him how he was doing with his large church, located not too far from where I lived.

"Oh, I guess it's going okay," Chris said rather absently. "Things are moving along pretty well."

Something about Chris's reply told me things weren't really that okay at all.

"Chris, how is it *really* going? Are you spending time—time with your wife and the children?"

And then he told me the truth. Just a few days before, his seven-year-old daughter had come home and told him, "Daddy, I never want to go into the ministry."

"Why, honey?" he asked.

"Because of you," the little girl said vehemently. "You're never home. You never do anything with us."

My chance encounter with Chris that day on the street led to my driving down to see him for a three-hour chat. As we talked, he said that he would soon be changing jobs, taking an administrative denominational position at the other end of the country. *Then* he'd have time to spend with the children.

"No, that's not true," I told him. "You've got to start now. Two nights a week at home, plus dates with your daughters after school, one hour for each girl every week. Chris, if you don't start making changes now, you never will, and if you don't change, you're going to lose your family. And if you can't change, get out of the ministry."

Chris gave me a startled look, but agreed that he would try. Before we parted, I also sketched out the rest of the Positive Parenting Plan, but emphasized that the plan is of little use unless a parent is present to use it.

Three months later I was running some errands and met a woman who attends Chris's church. She came up to me practically bubbling and said, "I can't thank you enough for what you have done in our church!"

"What do you mean?" I asked with a puzzled look. "I haven't spoken there for years."

"Oh, yes, you have," the woman corrected me. And then she told me about how Chris had gone back home and applied what we had talked about. As he became *available* to his family, they felt *accepted, appreciated,* and *loved.* For the first time, Chris became *accountable* to his wife and children, and they in turn responded to his *authority* as leader of the family, not because they had to, but because they wanted to. As Chris practiced the Six A's for Positive Parenting, he saw changes for the better. He shared with his congregation what was happening at home and it literally started to turn his church upside-down as other parents started doing the same things.

It Works for Us; It Will Work for You

What I told Chris isn't magic, nor is it some special insight sent from heaven. It is simple, biblical common sense anybody can put into practice. Dottie and I know it works because we've done it with our own children.

Several years ago, we decided we wanted to bring up our children in a small, rustic California town, about one hundred miles east of San Diego on the borders of the Cleveland National Forest. Because it's such a small community, everybody knows everybody else, and there isn't much you can hide from your neighbors.

From early on, the community has been well aware that Dottie and I keep a tight rein on our children. We have rules and we enforce them, but only after we communicate and hear their side.

For example, we're constantly evaluating the music they listen to and which concerts and movies they can attend. Other parents in town have come to trust our choices. Their children will come to them and say, "Can we go to such-and-such's concert?"

Often, they answer, "If Sean or Kelly McDowell can go, you can."

And then our children come to us and Kelly, for example, will say, "Daddy, my friends say they can go to the concert if I can go— can I?"

Sometimes we say yes, but more than half of the time we have to say no. That puts a lot of pressure on us, because we aren't only affecting our own children, but other children as well. We can come out looking like the "bad guys" who don't want kids to have any fun.

In one instance, after Sean had enrolled in a new Sunday school class, we heard second- and third-hand reports that his teacher was making comments about us—particularly me. This woman was the daughter of a Christian traveling evangelist who never had any time for his children—particularly her, the oldest child. This woman had grown up fully convinced that anyone involved in a traveling evangelism ministry like mine could never have decent family relationships. She was, of course, projecting her own problems as a young girl onto us and, while we regretted her attitude, there was little we could do about it.

The one who did do something about it was our son, Sean. As this woman watched Sean and heard him talk about his dad and mom, as well as his sisters, she realized that what she had said was wrong. She eventually came to Dottie and me to apologize and we developed an excellent relationship with her.

When a "C" Was Really an "A"

One of the best things about building a solid relationship with your children is that they will pick up your values and "live by the rules" because their values are your values. A few years ago, Kelly got a C on a history test. Because she was an A student, she was very upset, but when she told me the situation I realized how upset she really was and why.

It seems that a foreign student had taken that same history exam two weeks early, ahead of the rest of the class, and he had kept the questions. He gave them to several other students in the class and offered them to Kelly as well, but she said no. She'd get her grade on her own.

Kelly studied very hard, and after taking the exam she told me, "Daddy, that was the hardest test I have ever seen. I'm afraid I didn't do so well."

The grades came out and, sure enough, she got a C instead of her usual A. Three other A students in the class didn't do as well as Kelly and came out with C- or D grades. Strangely enough, however, two C students got A's on the exam. Of course, the two C students with A's were the same ones who had been given the test ahead of time. One of these C students only missed one question on the entire exam.

But as far as Dottie and I were concerned, Kelly's C was an A in our book. We were proud of what she had done on her own—getting an honest grade of C on one of the toughest exams she had ever seen in her life. And the best part of it was, she got a C, not because she wanted to obey our rules, but because she wanted to obey her own inner rules—to be honest and to earn any grade she got.

Saying "No" Is Hard, But Worth It

On another occasion, Kelly attended an eighth-grade graduation party at another student's home. As the evening went on, we got a call from Kelly saying she wanted to stay overnight. I listened to her request and then asked a few questions. Kelly admitted that there would be boys at the "extended" party and, no, she couldn't be positive there would be no drinking. When she told me the names of those who were planning to stay past ten o'clock, I recognized the name of one boy who had a reputation for being able to obtain alcohol, even though, like Kelly, he was only fourteen.

After hearing Kelly out, I replied, "No, Kelly, I don't think so. I want you to come home when the party ends at ten o'clock."

Kelly called back three times in the next half hour. At one point she began to cry, and then I learned what was really happening. Four or five of the other girls also wanted to stay overnight, but they had to get their parents' permission and everything depended on what Kelly McDowell's dad said.

It was obvious Kelly was getting pressured by her peer group. She began telling me there probably wasn't much to worry about. Parents would be in the house and there would be lots of kids around—nobody would be alone with anybody else.

I could tell Kelly was feeding me lines that her friends were giving her from the background, and I stuck with my original ruling. "Sorry, Kelly, but you'll have to come home. If you were a senior in high school, I might consider it—and then say no. But you're just going into ninth grade and Mom and I don't believe that all-night, co-ed parties are a very wise thing to do."

I hung up with my daughter's sniffles clearly ringing in my ears. I didn't like disappointing her, but I knew I had done the right thing. Later, when Kelly got home she woke us up and thanked us for telling her she couldn't stay overnight!

"Daddy," she said, "I didn't really want to stay, especially after you said no and the other girls started to pressure me. Thanks for helping me out."

Often, when Dottie or I make a stand and have to say no, our children thank us for having standards and sticking to them. Dick has had the same experience. In one case his sixteen-year-old son, Jonathan, asked him if he could attend a party where it was rumored there would be some drinking later on in the evening. Dick told Jonathan, "No, JJ, I don't think so. I don't want to be in the position of condoning that sort of thing."

Later, Jonathan thanked his dad for telling him no.

When parents make a stand and stick to their guns, I believe it does two things for their children: One, it helps them deal with the peer group because they can say, "I'm afraid my parents won't let me." Two, and even more important, it lets the child know that there are values and rules that can't be ignored or compromised.

I wouldn't want to claim for a minute that our children always accept our decisions gracefully or enthusiastically. There are times when we aren't thanked for saying no. But overall, our children obey the rules, not because they are afraid or because they're trying to fake obedience while they seethe on the inside. They obey the rules because of the relationship we have built with them ever since they were in the cradle.

The Bible Gives So Many Rules!

If you remember only one thing from this book, remember that *rules without relationships lead to rebellion*. Kids do not respond to rules; they respond to relationships.

"But, Josh," parents tell me, "I want to be biblical. The Bible lays down rules. Look at the Ten Commandments."

I agree, but then I point out that even the Ten Commandments were given in the context of a relationship that God had with His people. God knew that the Law alone would be too much for anyone to bear. What would save the Israelites would not be how well they obeyed the Ten Commandments, but their relationship to the Lord.

When the Israelites stood on the borders of Canaan, poised to go in and conquer the land, Moses addressed them and recalled the day they had provoked the Lord while he was on Mount Sinai, receiving the tablets containing the Ten Commandments. Moses reminded them of how they had decided to party while he was gone, how they had asked Aaron to make a golden calf, and how they had danced around it in a drunken orgy. Coming upon the scene, Moses had smashed the tablets containing the Ten Commandments and then spent thirty days praying day and night in intercession for his rebellious people.

The Lord heard Moses' prayer and withheld punishment. Instead, He instructed Moses to chisel out two more stone tablets like the first ones and then bring them to the mountain where He would again inscribe on them the same Ten Commandments He had written before.

As he summed up his story, Moses said: "And now, O Israel, what does the Lord God ask of you but to fear the Lord your God, to walk in all His ways, to love Him, to serve the Lord your God with all your heart and with all your soul, and to observe the Lord's commands and decrees that I am giving you today *for your own good?*" (see Deuteronomy 10:12–13, NIV, italics mine).

Rebellious as the Israelites could be, God always treated them like a loving father, doing everything "for their own good." The Ten Commandments were given to them as a safeguard and a blessing, not a burden. Although the law is perfect (Psalm 19:7), it becomes a teacher (Galatians 3:24) to show one's inadequacy in oneself. Yet love enables one to want to keep the law (Romans 13:10).

Many parents believe that they lay down rules and regulations for their children—particularly teen-agers—"for their own good," but what is missing is that relationship factor. Telling your children, "I'm doing this for your own good," will not cut it if they seldom see or hear you demonstrate the unconditional acceptance that makes them feel secure, the appreciation that makes them feel significant, the affection that makes them feel lovable. And if you aren't available to spend time and make your children feel important, you can't expect them to welcome your rules with open arms. Instead, you can usually expect rebellion of some kind.

I have many parents come to me when their kids are in their teens and in trouble—on drugs, sexually active, pregnant, involved in crime—every horror story you can think of. Their hearts are breaking and they ask, "What can we do?"

I often wish I could have talked with them before their kids were born, or at least when they were very young. That's the best time to start building a relationship that will pay off later. When children are teen-agers it's not too late, but it is much, much harder. It can take four or five years to build a relationship, and meanwhile, your teen-ager is going through the most turbulent time of his or her life. Still, it can be done. Remember: **It's never too late to start to build a relationship.**

Paul Knew Something about Kids, Too

The scholars differ on whether or not the apostle Paul was married, but he certainly knew plenty about raising children. In Colossians 3:20, Paul says something all parents dearly love: "Children, be obedient to your parents in all things, for this is well-pleasing to the Lord" (NASB). But what motivates children to obey their parents? In the next verse Paul adds, "Fathers, do not exasperate your children that they may not lose heart" (v. 21).

Have you ever been exasperated? Do you think exasperation is only an adult emotion? To exasperate means "to make very angry or irritated; tax the patience of; provoke; irk." And what is the result? The children can lose heart. In other words, they tell themselves: "What's the use? It doesn't matter what I do—it's never good enough. If my parents think I'm so bad, I might as well act that way!"

So how do you keep a child from becoming exasperated? Do you throw out all the rules and let the child run wild? No, that can be even more exasperating, because then the child thinks you don't care. Paul has the answer in Ephesians 6, a parallel passage to what he says in Colossians. Here he tells children to obey their parents because it is the right thing to do and adds, "Honor your father and mother (which is the first commandment with a promise), that it may be well with you and that you may live long on the earth."

Then he goes on, "And, fathers, do not provoke your children to anger; but bring them up in the discipline and instruction of the Lord" (Ephesians 6:1–4, NASB).*

Rules alone are not enough. You will wind up playing policeman as your children react in various negative ways. But when you provide loving acceptance and appreciation, demonstrated with liberal doses of affection and availability, your children will respond positively to rules. To put it in equation form:

---

* See chapter 14 for more on Ephesians 6:1–4 and how to be a relational parent.

Rules - a Relationship = Rebellion

Rules + a Relationship = Response

What parents always want to know is, "How can I have that kind of relationship with my kids? When I say no, they don't see me as a hero, but as an ogre. Where have I gone wrong?"

Instead of dwelling on how we can go wrong as parents, I want to pinpoint *how we can go right.* In the next few chapters we will explore the meaning of unconditional acceptance. Without your acceptance, your child's self-image shrinks and his self-esteem ebbs away. Specifically, what can you do to help your children know beyond any doubt that you love them no matter what they might do? To begin, we must go back to the source of all acceptance—God Himself.

To Think About, Discuss, or Try for Yourself

1. Take a few moments to analyze your relationship to your children. Rate your relationship to each child on a scale of 1 to 10, with 10 being excellent. Don't be surprised if you come up with different numbers for each one. Think about why that is true. Do certain of your children constantly complain about the rules? Do you have a hard time getting certain children to be obedient and cooperative? Think next about your relationship to any children you have who are "difficult." What is really causing this?

2. On page 29, Josh suggests to a Philippine pastor and father of three rebellious children that he should "forget the rules." What do you think that means? Is it really possible to put emphasis on the relationship and let the rules come afterward?

3. On page 30 Josh gives advice to Chris, a pastor whose little girl told him she never wanted to go into the ministry because he was never home and never did anything with her or the rest of the family. Josh's prescription was: two nights a week at home, plus dates with his children after school, one hour each, every week. Evaluate your own schedule. Do you spend certain nights at home with your family, taking time to interact with them, play games, wrestle, and so on? How many dates have you had with your children in the last month?

4. What happens when you face a situation with your child and decide you must say no? Do you hear your child out and then give your reasons, or are you more autocratic?

5. Are you doing anything that constantly provokes or exasperates your child? Why not sit down and talk with your child to see what he or she has to say?

Part II

Acceptance:
Builder of Security
and Self-worth

THE BEDROCK of any relationship is acceptance. Our relationship to God is based on His grace—His unconditional acceptance of us just as we are. We can do nothing to get God to love us. We come to Him in simple faith, trusting that He does love and accept us. Your child comes to you in much the same way. Is it possible to *unconditionally* love your child? Why do children need unconditional acceptance and what happens when they don't get it? What part does acceptance play in building the child's self-image and self-esteem? In this next section, we will learn the answers to these questions, plus . . .

- how to recognize when you are even subtly suggesting to your child that he or she must live on a performance basis

- where Scripture spells out each person's uniqueness and how you can treat your child as the unique person he or she is

- why "standardized parenting" doesn't work

- where concepts like "self-esteem" and "self-image" are clearly suggested and taught in Scripture

- the biblical definition of healthy self-esteem

- why some children may be led to think, "I'm not worth much, maybe I'm not worth anything"

- how to teach a child, "I'm made in God's image . . . I'm valuable—God don't make no junk!"

- some practical illustrations of how to communicate unconditional acceptance

- why acceptance is always a choice and how you can make that choice daily.

4

If You Accept Them, They'll Accept Themselves

Do you love your children because of what they do or because of who they are?

Take your time answering. If you give the question a little thought, the answer may not be as simple as it looked at first. A lot depends on what you understand and believe about unconditional acceptance versus conditional acceptance.

Unconditional acceptance is based on who your child is—a human being made in God's image, with value built-in by his Creator. Children parented with unconditional acceptance stand a much better chance of feeling good self-worth. They are much more likely to feel secure in their relationship with their parents. They usually respond well to loving authority. How important is unconditional acceptance?

Acceptance is all-important because it develops security, which makes a child willing to be vulnerable and transparent, opening up greater trust between you and your child.

On the other hand, conditional acceptance focuses on what the child does. If the child obeys, achieves, or performs well, he is accepted. But if his performance is not up to parental standards, he feels insecure, rejected, with a lack of self-worth and self-esteem. Willingness to be vulnerable and transparent fades along with trust between the two of you.

Insecurity Comes in Different Packages

In my travels, I am constantly meeting teen-agers and collegians who have known only conditional acceptance—or possibly very little acceptance at all.

Mark knows he can't ever get to college because when he was in grade school, one of his teachers told him he was stupid, and worse, his parents always told him, "You're lazy—you'll never amount to anything."

Lori grew up with her schoolmates teasing her unmercifully about her slender legs. Cries of "Bird legs!" and "You'd better wear skis in the shower" plagued her, even up through junior high. Today, as a junior in college, Lori is still slender while many of her classmates are already fighting weight problems. Yet she still apologies for her "skinny legs" and avoids appearing in a bathing suit.

Jeff comes across as self-assured and confident. He's at the top of his class and plays first string on the football team. Jeff's philosophy: "You've got to produce—otherwise, nobody thinks you're worth much."

In some people, like Mark and Lori, low self-esteem is easy to spot because they openly admit their insecurities and negative opinions of themselves. Others, like Jeff, try to hide their poor self-image with an aggressive, cock-sure attitude, but deep down they, too, are insecure and unsure.

"Unsure of what?" you may ask. Unsure that they are accepted— that they have worth and real value in themselves alone. Instead, they live life on a performance basis, believing they have to prove to others and to themselves that they do count, that they have any worth at all.

They believe they have to earn any acceptance they might get from others. They do not understand or believe that they have the same inborn rights shared by every human being made in God's image—to be loved and accepted simply for who they are, not what they do, how they look, or what they have.

Unfortunately, I find many young people who have fallen into the performance trap, right along with their parents and other adult role models. They fail to understand that God's unconditional love gives every human being worth. "What is man that You are mindful of him," writes the psalmist, "the son of man that You care for him? You made him a little lower than the heavenly beings and count him with glory and honor" (Psalm 8:4–5, NIV).

Is Self-esteem Biblical?

Ironically, I frequently meet people who doubt that self-esteem is a valid, biblical concept. After I finish speaking at a parents' seminar, I will often be challenged by a mother or father who will tell me that they are disturbed by my ideas concerning self-esteem. Perhaps they have read in a current best-selling book that self-esteem is a New Age concept—that it has nothing to do with being godly or biblical. From their reading, they have been convinced that desiring good self-esteem is sinful because it puts all your concentration on yourself. Whenever I am challenged in this way, I respond by saying something like this: "I appreciate your willingness to talk about this. While I agree that people can become self-centered and all wrapped up in their own self-interests, I don't agree that self-image and self-esteem are 'sinful' ideas. In fact, I believe that proper understanding of your self-image and self-esteem is exactly what keeps you from becoming selfish and self-centered."

As we discuss self-esteem and self-image, I usually recommend some reading, including my own book, *Building Your Self-Image* (Tyndale, Living Books, 1988), and an excellent book by Maurice Wagner, *The Sensation of Being Somebody* (Zondervan, 1975).

Let's Define "Self-Image" and "Self-Esteem"

All of us carry a mental picture of ourselves that is our self-image. Furthermore, research has born out that we will tend to act in harmony with whatever that mental self-portrait shows us. As a high school and college student, I certainly did. Because of my many difficulties at home, particularly with my father, plus my struggles with educators who would not accept my left-handedness and who viewed me as nothing more than a D student, my self-image was at rock bottom. I had few, if any, good feelings about myself.

It was through coming to a faith in Jesus Christ and realizing God's acceptance of me that I've been able to gain a healthy sense of self-worth. People with healthy self-worth can accept themselves, because they know God delights in and accepts them. Healthy self-worth believes, "I am lovable, worthy—a capable and competent part of God's creation. Yes, I am a sinner, but I've been redeemed by God. He has forgiven me for my sins and now I can become all He wants me to be."

People with a healthy sense of self-worth feel significant. They believe that they matter, that the world is a better place because they are there. A person with healthy self-worth can interact with others and appreciate their worth, too. This person can radiate hope, joy and trust. All this sounds strangely familiar—like what the Bible calls the fruit of the Spirit (Galatians 5:21–22).

Someone with a poor sense of self-worth, on the other hand, is a slave to the opinions of others. When you lack self-worth, you are not free to be yourself.

A student who appeared to be very secure wrote to me and confessed: "I think of myself as a turkey. I am so scared of what people think of me, it's hard to accept myself. I'm still afraid of looking people in the eye or even being around them. I feel like trash. My fear of rejection by others is great."[1]

Scripture Doesn't Teach Us to Put Ourselves Down

Christians who feel uneasy about acknowledging that they even have a self-image or any self-worth seem to be adamantly against the idea that they could love or accept themselves. Instead, they believe that they are insignificant worms, worthless sinners who deserve only hell-fire. Oddly enough, these people often quote a verse like Romans 12:3, "Do not think of yourself more highly than you ought, but rather think of yourself with sober judgment, in according to the measure of faith God has given you" (NIV). They believe this verse tells them not to think highly of themselves at all—that they should put themselves down.

But this verse says nothing about putting yourself down. What it does say is that we should think highly of ourselves as God's creation, but not more highly than what we really are. Paul is saying we should be realistic and use sober judgment. This verse provides the basis for a good biblical definition:

A healthy self-image:
"Seeing yourself as God sees you—no more and no less."

This means that we don't ignore the fact that we are sinners. But at the same time we don't dwell on that fact to the point of blocking out the Bible's clear declaration that we are made in God's image and, therefore, we have great built-in worth.

I Learned Early That Lefties Are Unacceptable

As I grew up, I knew nothing of being made in God's image and having intrinsic worth. I had no idea He accepted me, and I expended a lot of energy in trying to be accepted or "acceptable" to anyone who would listen. I was born a natural left-hander, and in my early grade-school years my teachers tried to force me to change to doing everything right-handed. One teacher, in particular, would stand over me with a ruler and slap my left hand if I tried to do anything with it.

"Think, Josh," she'd snap. "Use your right hand!"

It didn't take long for me to believe that left-handedness was inferior to right-handedness, and the logical conclusion was that I was inferior as well.

I became so nervous and insecure, I developed a speech impediment. Now my poor self-image and low self-esteem were compounded by my stutter.

It became difficult for me to do anything, especially speak in front of the class. One assignment called for all of us to recite the Gettysburg Address. I had it down cold at home and could say it without a hitch while cleaning the cow stalls, but in front of the class I froze. I began to stutter—couldn't even get out the first line—and finally ran from the classroom in embarrassment.

I Also Learned to Hate My Alcoholic Father

While school provided plenty of experiences that would erode my self-esteem, it was at home where the worst damage was done. I was always sure of my mother's love, but my terrible relationship with my alcoholic father almost destroyed me. By the time I was fourteen, my hatred of my father's drinking had turned into a hatred of him, which only increased as I went through high school.

One scene that is forever burned into my memory was the day that our senior class voted to have an end-of-the-year picnic at our farm. We were all having a great time, until my father turned into our driveway. His old pickup weaved back and forth, kicking up clouds of dust as he barely avoided hitting a tree, a fence, and our dog.

My father stopped the pickup, got out, and staggered toward the house, nearly falling several times. When my friends saw that he was drunk—again—they laughed and made jokes. I had to run to the barn and stay there for awhile, because I was just too ashamed to face them.

My Mother Died of a Broken Heart

Two months before my high school graduation, I came home from a date around midnight to find my mother weeping bitterly.

"What's wrong? What happened?" I demanded, thinking that perhaps my father had beaten her again. After several minutes, she finally gained enough composure to talk.

"It's all too much . . . I can't take it anymore," she sobbed. "Your father . . . his drinking . . . the abuse. . . ."

"I know, Mom," was all I could manage.

"I can't take it any more," she cried. "I . . . I've lost the will to live. I want to wait until you're on your own after graduation next month . . ." more uncontrollable sobs, "then I just want to die."

This wasn't the first time my mother had talked this way. But this time there was something different. It was almost as if she were predicting her death. Was she hinting about suicide? I couldn't tell for sure, but her outburst frightened me.

Two months later I graduated from high school, and on the following Friday my mother died. Can a person die of a broken heart? Physically, I suppose the answer is no. But mentally and emotionally the answer is definitely yes. My mother died, her self-esteem and self-image ripped asunder by my father's treatment. When my mother died, I lost my last real source of security and stability. No matter where I would go, or how late I would come home, my mother had always been there, waiting for me, wanting to talk to me, interested in my life. Now she was gone, and I was alone.

I Arrived at College Spiritually Bankrupt

During the funeral, I stared at my father, my eyes smoldering with hatred. I despised him and eventually I probably would have done something desperate had I not left home to go to college. I chose a small, secular school and arrived on campus, emotionally and spiritually bankrupt. I longed for unconditional, unstoppable love. I desperately wanted to be accepted by others, but I was even more desperate about wanting to be able to accept myself and overcome my feelings of self-loathing.

I wanted the things all young people look for—security, confidence, peace of heart and mind—and, oh, yes, happiness. I made a project out of trying to find happiness, and during my freshman year I tried to lose myself in becoming a big leader on campus. I was elected freshman class president and was soon taking part in heady decision-making, such as which speakers to invite to campus and what kind of parties to throw with student money.

My routine turned into the drudgery of classes from Monday through Friday, with happiness revolving around three nights: Friday, Saturday, and Sunday.

As the weeks went by, I began noticing a small group of students, about eight in all, who seemed to spend a lot of time with two faculty members. I couldn't put my finger on it, but there was something different about them. They knew what they believed and why, and I had always admired that quality in anyone. They also seemed to have a sense of direction, something sadly lacking in most of the people I was running with. Most unusual of all, they often talked about love and went out of their way to help others, a very rare commodity on a secular college campus.

I wanted to know just exactly what made these people tick, so I decided to make friends with them. They challenged me to examine on an intellectual basis what they believed about Jesus Christ.

My study took almost two years, but when I was through, I was no longer a skeptical agnostic. The evidence I uncovered convinced me that Jesus Christ is Who He claimed to be—the Son of God and the Savior of the world. Confronted with that evidence, I wrestled with the next challenge—becoming a Christian. Much like C. S. Lewis, I was dragged kicking and screaming into God's kingdom, and I finally committed my life to Jesus Christ.

And over a period of time, Christ did change my life. For the first time I felt real security, self-worth—and peace. Because Jesus had taken the penalty for my sins, I knew that God had accepted me just the way I was. I couldn't do anything to earn His acceptance. He was giving me salvation only because of my faith—nothing else.

God's unconditional acceptance is a tremendous truth that often is overlooked. Like Mark, Lisa, and Jeff, mentioned earlier in this chapter, people get hung up on their appearance or their lack of ability, talent, or possessions. They go through life trying to earn acceptance, not realizing that they have already been accepted by God Himself. Strictly on the marvelous merits of Jesus Christ alone, God accepts you and me and our children, exactly the way we are, no strings attached. That's what John meant when he wrote, "This is love: not that we loved God, but that He loved us and sent His Son as an atoning sacrifice for our sins" (1 John. 4:10, NIV).

As the Bible's truths sank into my soul, I slowly realized it was a fallacy to think I had to be perfect to be acceptable, that I had to perform at a certain standard and keep everybody impressed. Eventually it didn't matter any more that I was left-handed or that I had stuttered as a child and still stuttered on occasion when I got nervous. All of that negative conditioning slowly melted away, and so did my desire to cover up my deficiencies and weaknesses. I could admit I wasn't perfect, but, paradoxically, I also understood that I was "perfect in Jesus Christ," and that made all the difference.

God Changed My Father, Too!

Through my new-found faith, I realized that God's acceptance could fill the void I had felt all my life because my father hadn't accepted me. But God wasn't through, and He sent along a little "bonus."

After becoming a Christian, I tried to develop a better relationship with my father, but I didn't make much progress. Then one day, while driving alone, I stopped at a train crossing and got rear-ended by a drunken driver traveling over forty miles per hour. I wound up in the hospital with both legs, an arm, and my neck in traction. When I finally came home, my father, totally sober for once, came to my room and said, "How in the world can you love a father such as I?"

"Dad," I said, "six months ago I despised you, but Christ has changed my life." Then I shared with him what I had discovered about Jesus Christ.

My dad didn't argue. He just listened quietly. Then and there he prayed with me, and I could hardly believe what I was hearing: "God, if You really are God and Christ is Your Son, and You can do in my life what You've done in my son's life, I want You as my personal Savior."

A few months later, I was able to go back to school and I transferred to a college in Michigan, not far from my dad's farm. My father had never remarried after my mother died, but he did date occasionally. Sometimes he'd come up to see me at college and we'd go on double dates together.

After all the years of grief and misery, my father and I had fourteen great months before a heart attack took him home. Those fourteen months taught me that it's never too late to make up for lost time. It's never too late to start accepting one another. What I experienced with my dad during that last year he had on this earth has never stopped motivating me to have the best possible relationship I can with my own children.

The Accepted Child Accepts Himself

I have taken time to tell you about my own struggles with lack of good self-image and healthy self-esteem to illustrate how critical it is for a child to feel accepted, particularly by role models like his parents or his teachers. If all a child seems to hear is that what he is doing is wrong, the child naturally concludes, "I'm not worth much—maybe I'm not worth *anything.*"

Feeling unaccepted by those most important to him, the child refuses to accept himself, which is the root problem of poor self-image and weak self-esteem.

At the opposite end of the spectrum is the child who feels special because his parents have made him or her feel that way. Dottie's parents had a knack for this. They could make each of their three children feel special, but none of them ever felt that one was more special than the other. Dottie has often told me that it would have made her feel very uncomfortable and even resentful if somehow she thought she was the favorite or that her brother or sister was the favorite.

While Dottie's parents loved their children equally, they had simple ways to recognize each child as an individual. Dottie's dad would say to her, "You're my favorite big girl." Then he would say to her sister Sally, seven years younger, "You're my favorite little girl." And to her brother, Steve, he would say, "You're my favorite boy."

Dottie has carried on that practice with our children. Kelly is her "favorite big girl." Sean is her "favorite boy," Katie her "favorite blonde," Heather her "favorite black-eyed kid."

It's a simple little device, but it works. Sean, for example, knows that he's the only boy in the family, but he still likes to hear that he's "our favorite boy." The point is, there are ways to make each child feel special, and you need to develop the techniques that work best with your children.

Dottie corresponds occasionally with a friend who has two sons born quite close together. This woman writes glowingly about one son, calling him her pride and joy, but she rarely mentions the other. The favoritism is obvious, and we can only wonder what it may be doing to the boy who is not the favorite.

In his fine book, *Hide or Seek,* Dr. James Dobson points out that an epidemic of inferiority has swept through a large percentage of people in twentieth-century America. But he believes that the epidemic can be stopped by parents who subscribe completely to the proposition that all children are created equally worthy and must be given the right to personal respect and dignity.

I believe Dr. Dobson is saying only what the Bible says. It is every parent's task to give his child a healthy sense of personal self-worth, and every parent who does so will be a hero to his kids in the truest sense of the word!

To Think About, Discuss, or Try for Yourself

1.   Specifically, how can you as a parent build your child's self esteem? One place to start is to talk informally with your child about what the Bible says:

- We are created in God's image (Genesis 1:26–27)

- God has given us a special purpose—to subdue (manage) the earth (Genesis 1:28)

- We have been made "a little lower than the angels" (Psalm 8:5)

- Everyone has sinned and come short of the glory of God (Romans 3:23), *but* God sent His only Son to die for our sins (John 3:16)

- Each of us has the potential to become a child of God through believing on the name of Jesus Christ (John 1:12–13)

- God redeemed (bought us) at the highest price He could possibly pay—the death of His Son on the cross (1 Corinthians 6:20, 1 Peter 1:18–19)

- Because we are redeemed, angels watch over us (Hebrews 1:14, Psalm 91:11–12)

- Jesus Himself is preparing a place for us where we can be with Him always (John 14:1–3)

Perhaps you yourself haven't experienced the reality of these scriptural truths. Think about them, pray about them, talk with your pastor or a Christian friend in whom you can confide. As these truths become more and more real for you, you can share them with your children with conviction and enthusiasm. What better way would there be to start teaching them about acceptance? What better way would there be to let them know that they are accepted by God and Jesus Christ and that you accept them as well?

I also suggest that you get a copy of my book, *Building Your Self-Image,* which is available in paperback through Tyndale House Publishers (Living Books Edition). Read it, study it, and complete the "Building Block" exercises. Learning how to have a healthy, biblical view of yourself will make it easier to pass these truths on to your children.

2.   Talking with your children about biblical truths can help them begin to feel accepted, but if these truths are to come alive, *your kids*

need to see frequent demonstrations by Mom and Dad. Some Christian parents make a vital mistake, often through carelessness or by default, of teaching their children the Bible *but not role-modeling what the Bible means.* The result is that their children grow up learning the "party line." They learn all the right words and phrases, but see little of all this actually being done by the people who matter the most in their lives—their parents.

Why not stop right now and take an objective inventory of your own family? Are your children simply hearing the Bible and being told the rules, or are they experiencing the Bible's truth because their parents treat them and each other according to what Scripture teaches? Talk together with your spouse about how well both of you are role-modeling biblical truth before your children. Then take time to pray together for wisdom to do it better.

5

Acceptance: The Real Meaning of Proverbs 22:6

WHEN MY son Sean was twelve, he played on a Little League baseball team. A week before the season started, I got an idea about how to show him—and his teammates—acceptance. I bought twelve coupons good for ice cream sundaes at a local restaurant, and took them to his coach.

"Coach, these are for the kids," I said.

"Good," the coach said with a big smile. "This is great. I wish more dads took an interest like this. I'll take them for sundaes after our first win."

"No, Coach," I said quickly. "I want you to take them for sundaes after their first *loss*."

Sean's coach looked at me strangely. What I was saying wasn't computing with his concept of winning, losing, and rewards for good play. This is what I shared with him:

"Coach, I don't know about you, but as I raise my kids I don't want to acknowledge their success as much as their effort. And I don't want to acknowledge their effort as much as their being created in the image of God. I believe my son is created in the image of God and that he has infinite value, dignity, and worth, which all have nothing to do with playing baseball. If he never played baseball an inning in his life, I would love and accept him just as much."

Sean's coach looked at me for a long moment. Finally, all he could muster was, "Well, *that's novel.*"

The season started and Sean's team won their first few games. But they lost the third or fourth game, and the coach was true to his word. He gave each player an ice cream sundae coupon and they all went out to "celebrate" their loss.

Sean must have thanked me at least five times for the sundaes. In addition, over the next two weeks three of the kids on his team came up and thanked me for the special treat. I recall especially a boy named Jessie, who said, "Thanks a lot for the ice cream sundaes, Mr. McDowell. Wow! It doesn't matter to you if we win or not—you love us anyway."

Nothing could have made me happier than to hear that. What I wanted to communicate to Sean and his teammates is that their worth is not based upon their ability to play baseball. It's based upon the fact that they are each created in the image of God with infinite value and infinite dignity. Is that kind of lesson too difficult for a twelve-year-old to grasp? Obviously not, especially when you use ice cream to prove your point!

You Are One in Five Billion

I also want Sean—and all my kids—to know that along with creating us in His image, God created each of us as *unique individuals.* Think of it: of the over five billion people alive right now on planet earth, there is no one just like you. And there is no one just like your son or your daughter.

I often ask students, "If out of five billion people, there is only one you, why in the world would you want to be like someone else?"

Yet, many people do want to be someone else. They go through life envying others—their physique, their hair, their complexion, their talents, their abilities. A starting point for building a healthy self-image is to fix your thoughts on the fact that God made you unique. And to paraphrase the well-known bumper sticker: **"God Don't Make No Junk."**

One of the best descriptions of a child's uniqueness is found in some familiar words penned by King Solomon: "Train up a child in the way he should go, even when he is old he will not depart from it" (Proverbs 22:6, NASB).

Unfortunately, this verse is often misunderstood by Christian parents who think it means, "Have family devotions, take children to Sunday school and church, and when they are grown up, they'll not depart from the faith."

The real meaning of this verse, however, centers on that phrase "according to his way." The writer is referring to the *child's* way, not God's. The root meaning of these words suggests "stimulating a desire for guidance according to one's own uniqueness."

Over in the Psalms, the same Hebrew word is translated "bend," and refers to the bending of an archer's bow. Today, with precision manufacturing, almost anyone can pick up a forty-five-pound bow and do a great job of hitting the target. But in biblical days, nothing was standardized. An archer had to use his own bow and become very familiar with its strength and other qualities.

Every archer made his own bow and had to know the unique characteristics of that bow if he hoped to hit anything with it.

In the same way, every parent needs to know the unique characteristics of each child in the family. Training up each child in "his own way" doesn't mean you let a child run wild or allow him to get his own way all the time. In the *Ryrie Study Bible,* a note on Proverbs 22:6 explains that "in the way he should go" really means "according to his way; i.e., the child's habits and interests. The instruction must take into account his individuality and inclinations, and be in keeping with his physical and mental development."[1]

Just as an archer would find the particular "bend of his bow," you must find the particular bend of each of your children. Parents know instinctively that each of their kids is different, but they still often make the mistake of disciplining all their children in essentially the same way. Perhaps this comes from having the same expectations for all of the children. I agree that all families need standards by which to operate, but there is no standard way to treat all children because each child responds differently to how he or she is treated. In fact:

**"Standardized Parenting" is the
best way to ruin all children.**

Why a Child's Earliest Years Are So Crucial

Dick and Charlotte have had such an impact on my life in this area of parenting. I first learned of the psychology of parenting from watching them with their own children, and then began to use those principles as Dottie and I started our own family.

According to psychologist Erik Erikson, recognized as a leading authority in the field of human development, all of us pass through eight "ages" or stages of development during our lives. For the first two years, a child is in the age of *trust* as his parents provide for his simplest basic needs. It is during this time that the foundations of his self-image and feelings of security are laid.

Next, the child moves into the age of *autonomy,* which is characterized by the typical two-year-old's insistence on "Me! Mine!" Now the child begins to see himself as a unique being rather than the extension of everything else. Now is when his parents need to start recognizing his uniqueness and begin training him up "in his own way." In other words, start recognizing the child's individual personality and work with it to teach and nurture.

As the child reaches preschool years and starts interacting with other children in day care or preschool settings, he moves into the age of *initiative.* Up to this point, toddlers have engaged in "parallel play," meaning that they play individually alongside each other, but not really together. As the toddler moves into preschool (ages three to five), he begins to interact and play with other children. Now the child begins taking some initiative. He starts to make things cooperatively, to join with other children to plan and construct.[2]

All of these first three stages are crucial to the formation of a child's self-image. We often hear about the importance of the first three to five years of a child's life. Parents cannot start too young to recognize how special each child is and to nurture that specialness through unconditional acceptance in every way that they can. As Dr. Howard Hendricks' wife, Jean, put it when Dottie heard her speak many years ago:

**When it comes to children, it's important as a parent
to cooperate with nature.**

There Is No One Else Like Your Child

It is an awesome responsibility to find out what each child is like and bring that child up accordingly. In our home, we discipline one child one way and another child in a totally different manner. For example, if I would decide to discipline Kelly by making her sit in the center of the room for a half hour, or perhaps even longer, it would have no effect. She wouldn't mind at all because she would just make up games in her mind and have the greatest time in all the world.

On the other hand, sitting in the middle of the room for even twenty minutes was "horrible punishment" to Sean. Sean is a people person and can't stand being away from people for any length of time. To require Sean to sit with no one to talk to and "nothing to do" would result in immediate behavioral change. And when it comes to Heather and Katie, we have to use a different system entirely.

That's just one simple example from my family. If you start studying your own children, you will find dozens of ways each one is unique. Be sure to communicate the glories and wonder of that uniqueness to your child *positively* as well as to use it for correction.

It is important to accept your uniqueness and be happy with who God created you to be instead of always trying to be somebody else. I have never seen this thought put better than in a poem by Byron Michow, a college student at Penn State who heard me speak on this subject. Afterward, he wrote the following, which he simply entitled "Me."

> All my life I've tried to please others.
> All my life I've put on an act for others.
>> I will not do this.
> For if I spend my time trying to be someone else,
>> Who will spend time being me?

To build a child's self-image and accept their specialness, constantly remind him or her: "If there is no one else like you, why not be the unique you that God created in the first place? You are the best *you* there will ever be!"

God Knows Us Best and Loves Us Most

Right along with constantly reinforcing your child's uniqueness, let your child know that he or she is special and loved very much. God says so, and we can take Him at His word. Through Jeremiah, God said: "I have loved you with an everlasting love; I have drawn you with loving-kindness" (Jeremiah 31:3, NIV).

And in Romans 8, Paul guarantees God's future love, no matter what trials and hardships may come our way, when he states that nothing—absolutely nothing—can separate you or me or our children from the love of God (vs. 38–39).

I talk to a lot of people, young and old, who don't realize that God loved them even before they became Christians. While we were in darkness and His enemies, while we were yet sinners, He loved us and died for us (see Ephesians 5:8, Romans 5:8). If He loved us when we didn't have a personal relationship with Him, how much more does He love us now as His adopted children? Jesus gives us a very good clue when He says, "As the Father has loved me, so have I loved you. Now remain in My love" (John 15:9, NIV).

I can recall a day when a phrase from a song by Bill and Gloria Gaither seemed to jump off the page and speak directly to me: "I am loved. I am loved . . . *the One Who knows me best loves me most*" (italics mine).[3]

God knows all of us through and through. I often thank God for these startling words from Psalm 139: "O, Lord, You have searched me and You know me . . . You are familiar with all my ways. Before a word is in my tongue, You know it completely, O, Lord" (vs. 1, 3–4).

The psalmist is saying that God knows me better than my wife, Dottie, knows me, that He knows me better than anyone else in the universe. He knows my very thoughts even before I think them, and still He accepts me completely without the slightest reservation or condition.

And the same is true for everyone. Here is a truth to communicate to your children in every way you can, as often as possible. The same God Who knows you and me best, loves us most!

I take time here to mention God's love and acceptance because I know that many parents struggle with their own lack of a good self-image and healthy self-esteem. You may have been brought up in a home where you found little acceptance or, if you got acceptance, it was on a performance (conditional) basis. But because you may have been reared in a less-than-perfect atmosphere doesn't mean that you can't break the cycle with your own children.

If reading this book communicates only one point to you, Dick and I hope that it is the realization that you are accepted by God, unconditionally, and that He will empower you to accept your children unconditionally as well. That doesn't mean that you have to be perfect. That doesn't mean you won't ever get frustrated or angry with your children at times for their behavior. No human being can show perfect patience and total unconditional acceptance. God is the only One capable of that. But God, our great role model, is also our great source of power and energy to accept our children *less conditionally* and prove to them that they don't have to earn their acceptance or self-worth.

Accepting Kelly—and Jim Bakker

When my daughter Kelly was thirteen, she gave me a golden opportunity to tell her that I love her for who she is, not what she does—or doesn't do.

I picked her up one day after school and decided to meet her at the door as she came out. As we walked across the parking lot to the car, she asked, "Daddy, what do you think of Jim Bakker?"

Jim and Tammy Bakker had been all over the news, but I had no idea that they had become discussion material for a secular junior high classroom. Whenever I get a tough question from my kids, I often answer their question with a question of my own. This gives me a context that helps my thinking. (It also helps me stall for time to think of an answer.)

"Why do you ask?" I responded.

"Oh, in class today we spent an entire hour talking about Jim Bakker and everything he did with Jessica Hahn and all . . . I just wondered what you thought about what he did."

All kinds of responses flashed through my mind. I thought about what most Christian parents, and even non-Christians, might have said: "Oh, I think it's awful. I think it's disgusting. They ought to throw them out of the ministry . . . he's probably not even a real Christian!"

I had already been hearing pastors say this very kind of thing to their congregations and, while I understood their outrage, I also realized something else. Any pastor saying things like that about Jim Bakker was only succeeding in telling the young people in his church: "If you ever get in trouble, don't come to me as your pastor." In particular, he was sending to all the teen-age girls in the congregation this message: "As your pastor, I'll love and accept you, if you stay pure, but if you get pregnant out of wedlock, I'll condemn you."

And Christian parents who spoke about Jim Bakker in negative, judgmental terms were only managing to communicate to their own kids: "We only love and accept you if you don't get on drugs, if you don't drink, if you don't get pregnant."

And so, how would I answer? How could I walk the line between telling my thirteen-year-old daughter what I thought of sin, without condemning the sinner? I swallowed hard, bit my lip, and said: "Honey, what Jim Bakker did was wrong. It was sin."

Then I took time to explain to Kelly why it was sin, what it actually meant for Jim Bakker to meet Jessica Hahn in that hotel room. And then I went on:

"But, Kelly, you need to realize something. Everyone in your class needs to realize that God loves Jim Bakker as much as He loves you or me. Everyone needs to realize that Christ died for Jim Bakker as much as He died for you and me. If God can't forgive Jim Bakker, then He can't forgive you or me."

As we continued walking across the parking lot toward the car, Kelly said nothing for a few moments. As we walked along, I tried to think of how to put into words what I really wanted to say to her: *I don't love you because you're a virgin. If you ever get pregnant you can come to your dad because, just as I want to minister the grace of God to Jim Bakker, I want to minister the grace of God to you, my daughter.*

Taking a deep breath, I stopped Kelly, turned her face toward mine and said, "Honey, let's look at this realistically. If you got pregnant, can you imagine what your dad would go through? I'd get crucified. Half the people here in our own church would turn on me. All over the country, Christian leaders, magazine editors, reporters, evangelists—they'd all have me for lunch."

Kelly looked up at me, her blue eyes wide with concern and said, "I know it, Dad."

"But honey, I want you to know one thing," I continued. "If you ever did get pregnant, I wouldn't care what the people in our home church would say. I wouldn't care what all the evangelists, pastors, Christian leaders, magazine editors, and anybody else would say. I'd turn my back on all that, but I'd never turn my back on you. I'd put my arms around you and we'd see it through together."

At that moment, my thirteen-year-old daughter dropped her books, right on the parking lot pavement, started crying, threw her arms around me, and exclaimed, "I know you would, Daddy!"

"Well," I said with a chuckle, "I'm just going to keep reminding you." To myself, I thought, *And I'm going to keep reminding myself of what I said this day.*

That encounter happened several years ago. Since Kelly and I had that first talk about what I thought of Jim Bakker, I've made it a point to remind her on various occasions that I accept her, that I trust her, and that I love her no matter what might happen. Some people might think I'm taking too big a risk and that perhaps Kelly might "take me up on my offer." Or she might get careless, thinking, "It doesn't matter—Dad will love me anyway." But I don't worry about that, because I do trust her and I know that our relationship is strong.

But what would I do, God forbid, if something like pregnancy out of wedlock might happen with Kelly or Katie or Heather? It would be a shocker, but I can only pray that if that time comes, God will give me the grace to be the kind of father he designed me to be. And I believe He would give me the strength and the love to put my arms around my daughter and we would see it through together.

Accepting Tinker Bell and Her Pixie Dust

Being able to accept your child in a heavy crisis, such as "Mom, I'm pregnant," depends on how well you accept him or her in the more common everyday things that are part of growing up. In chapter 1, I mentioned how impressed I was when I started dating Dottie and got to meet her parents. They showed her their acceptance in dozens of ways, and I soon learned that it wasn't a special act they were putting on for my benefit.

Dottie's mother, in particular, had an incredible knack of being able to delight in her children. She could verbally express her joy to her children and show it with her body language—in every way that she acted. She could enter into their world and see life through their eyes. She could jump into their minds and understand their perspective.

For example, when Dottie was around seven years old, one of her favorite stories at the time was Peter Pan. She liked to live in her own fantasy world, acting out the various characters in the Peter Pan story. One day, while her mother was doing something in another part of the house, Dottie slipped down to the basement and found a huge box of Ivory Snow. As Dottie ran the Ivory Snow through her fingers, she began to think of the pixie dust that Tinker Bell used in the story of Peter Pan.

"I'll be Tinker Bell and spread my pixie dust everywhere," seven-year-old Dottie told herself. She walked around the basement, flinging handfuls of Ivory Snow in the air, and soon "pixie dust" covered everything. For a few moments Dottie was in shear ecstasy, lost in her Peter Pan fantasy. Then she looked around and suddenly realized what a mess she had made. All she could think of was, "Oh, boy. . . ."

Sure enough, her mother happened along a few minutes later and discovered the mess. You wouldn't blame a busy mom for hitting the roof at a moment like that, but Dottie recalls what happened like this:

"Mom reacted much differently. She entered into my world and understood the delight and ecstacy that I had felt when I was Tinker Bell spreading my pixie dust everywhere. She sat down and cuddled me and we talked about Peter Pan and all of his adventures. She entered into my dreams and let me relive my feelings. We laughed about the pixie dust that was everywhere and then we cleaned it all up together."

I love this little story about Dottie and her pixie dust because it so beautifully illustrates what acceptance is all about. Dottie's mother didn't accept the mess. In fact, she let Dottie know that it was indeed a mess and they'd better get it cleaned up as quickly as they could. But at the same time, she didn't destroy the wonderful feeling that Dottie had from her experience. Instead of clobbering Dottie or bawling her out, she lived something out with her daughter that was very important.

The pixie dust escapade is just one example of countless times Dottie can remember how her mother would express her acceptance and delight in her children. She wasn't permissive and didn't let her kids get away with anything they pleased. She always let them know what was right and wrong, but *she always put her acceptance ahead of everything else*.

Dottie grew up hearing her mother say, "Being a mom is the most fulfilling thing that I have ever done. There is nothing I would rather do than be your mom."

An Unaccepted Child Lives in Fear

Something I noticed immediately when I met Dottie and we started dating was how secure she was as a person. After I heard a few "pixie dust" stories I understood why. Dottie is living proof that a parent's loving acceptance builds security in a child. After Dottie and I married and our children began arriving, I often marveled at how she worked at accepting them. She was a role model for me and I learned much about accepting our kids from watching my wife.

I can't begin to count how often our acceptance of our children has paid off as they have grown up in our home. There is *nothing* more important for a parent to learn and practice than unconditional acceptance. You see, if your child does not feel your unconditional acceptance, your child will not feel secure. An insecure child is seldom willing to be vulnerable. The insecure child will not be transparent. That is, he will not come home from school to share with you what's been happening, what his friends have been doing and saying. If a child feels unaccepted and insecure, the child lives in fear—the fear that "I'll be rejected so I'd better keep my mouth shut."

That's why acceptance must come first in building your relationship with your children. The more you can communicate unconditional acceptance to your children, the more prone they will be to be open, to share and tell you what's happening in their lives.

As I said earlier, unconditional acceptance isn't easy. If we want to be honest, it isn't even totally possible. Only God can be totally unconditionally accepting. As a fallen sinner, I am limited, but I believe I am constantly growing toward God's ideal.

There are times when one of my kids does something and I have to bite my lip, take a deep breath, and maybe even go for a short walk. Because I have a tendency to discipline them too severely—I'm especially prone to "overgrounding." Then I have to come back later, reduce the penalties and apologize. But any weaknesses I have in practicing unconditional acceptance are vastly outweighed by the power of the Holy Spirit, Who gives me abilities that I didn't even know I had.

To recap what we've been saying in these first chapters, rules without relationships lead to rebellion. But as you build a good relationship—based upon your acceptance of your child—you won't face rebellion. Instead, you will get your child's response. It might not always be as obedient or as sweet as you would like, but it will be a response made in trust, not fear, because your child will know beyond all doubt that *whatever happens* you love him or her.

This certainty of your love has to be built on that foundation of your acceptance. The same is true with God's love for us. Some scholars believe that the apostle Paul's deepest thinking about the nature of the church was done in his letter to the Ephesians. What Paul says about the church—the worldwide family of believers—applies to your family as well. As Paul opens his letter, he tells the

Ephesian Christians that God's ". . . unchanging plan has been to adopt us into His own family by sending Jesus Christ to die for us. And He did this *because He wanted to!*" (Ephesians 1:5, TLB, italics mine).

God accepts us because He wants to, not because He has to. Acceptance is always a choice. In the next chapter, Dick Day will share how he learned this truth in a tiny country thousands of miles from home, and how that lesson changed him and his family forever.

To Think About, Discuss, or Try for Yourself

1.   This chapter opens with a story of how Josh provided ice cream sundaes for his son's team after their *first loss.* Have you ever celebrated with your children after they have lost a Little League game or some other contest? Why not try it and see what happens?

2.   In what ways are you trying to discover your child's bent—that is, his or her true personality, interests, and talents? Talk with your spouse about the possible dangers of slipping into "standardized parenting"—treating all the children exactly alike all of the time. Discuss which children in your family need what treatment and why. Encourage one another to parent them accordingly.

3.   What if your daughter got pregnant or your son "got a girl in trouble"? Could they come to you and tell the truth without fear of your rejection? Have you ever told them as much?

4.   Think of several things you can do or say in the coming week that will remind your child, "*You* are the best *you* there will ever be!"

5.   Do you identify with Josh when he mentions that accepting his children is not always easy, that at times he has to bite his lip, take a deep breath, and go for a walk? On whom does he rely to help him during moments of weakness? Make the following your daily prayer:

"Lord, help me remember this day that You accept me unconditionally and, whatever happens, I want to accept my children in the same way, as You give me the strength and the wisdom."

6

Acceptance Says, "You're Somebody Special"
(Dick Day)

FOR SEVERAL years I was engaged in private family counseling in the affluent community of Newport Beach, California. One of my most challenging clients was a young woman in her mid-thirties who desperately needed love and acceptance. The only problem was she didn't want to talk about love or about God, the source of all love and acceptance.

Janet, an only child, had grown up in a home with a demanding autocratic father, who always made her feel she was not doing enough—even *being* enough. An autocrat is a domineering, arrogant ruler who has absolute and unrestricted power. Her father fit this description perfectly, and he used this power in the ultimately despicable sense by physically and sexually abusing his daughter.

I noticed immediately that the moment I would mention God, Janet would stiffen and a cloud would come over her face. The word "God" suggested a father figure and that made her think of her natural father. Instantly, all of the horror, aches, and despair from her childhood would well up within her.

Likewise, the word "love" provoked strong emotions, but not in a positive way. Because she had received no love at all from her father—only abuse—she had given herself to any number of young men, just so they'd say, "I love you." Of course, these young men were more than happy to oblige in order to get what they wanted. They told her "I love you" to use and abuse her. So even the word "love" had much hurt associated with it.

All her life, Janet had received nothing, while others, particularly men, had taken whatever they wanted.

At home, all Janet had known were the limits and dictates of her autocratic, domineering father, which were pushed to horrifying extremes by her father's sexual abuse. Janet's rebellion against fathers, earthly and heavenly, and the giving of her body and soul to any young man who would have her is no mystery. She was an extreme case of what happens when life gets so totally out of balance.

The only way I could work with Janet was to help her realize that God was a loving heavenly Father and not at all like her weak, mixed-up, and corrupt natural father. To establish some kind of contact, I did something that probably would have caused a lot of my good Christian friends to think that I had gone a bit liberal. I began talking with Janet about the "Being" who liked her. I took on the role of a comforting counselor-father image, not to bring her to me, but to bring her *through* me, one in the image of God, to the heavenly Father, a role God intended for natural fathers and mothers. Eventually, as I showed her acceptance and appreciation, I had the complete freedom to speak of God and His love. I personally had the joy of seeing Janet respond not only to my counsel, but to the love of God, as well.

Rebellion Says, "Please Notice, Please Love Me!"

When a person feels unaccepted, rebellion springs up in various forms. Janet was an extreme case, but you can see the results of feeling unaccepted in all kinds of settings. For example, while in private practice I spent some time counseling in the public schools. Part of my duties included training teachers how to supervise the schoolyard during recess. These teachers told me that between 80 and 90 percent of all misbehavior on the playground would take place within ten yards of them. This seemed odd to many of my trainees. They thought children would misbehave at a far end of the playground where they weren't so likely to be seen.

Not so. I explained to the teachers that what the kids were saying was, "Hey, I'm here. I want love. And if I can't have love, I want attention—and I will do anything to get it." These children weren't getting love at home—they weren't even getting hate. One must be involved to hate, and their parents were not involved. They were indifferent to their children. The greatest affront to the dignity of any person is to treat them as if they are not significant, as if they do not even exist.

This kind of behavior was true from kindergarten through eighth grade, but it could have been just as true had the school included ninth through twelfth grade. The misbehavior of high school students might be a little more sophisticated, but it would still be there.

The point is, *everyone wants to be accepted,* especially children. If they don't get acceptance one way, they'll try another, even if what they try is "unacceptable" to those around them. Why is this true?

Josh and I believe the answer lies in how God created human beings and how He relates to them. We put such importance on acceptance because it is obviously God's first building block in developing the human personality. God, the heavenly Father, wants to change the behavior of His children, but before He endeavors to change us, He first of all meets us right where we are—through grace. And what is grace? Unconditional acceptance. The Bible clearly teaches us that we don't have to change to be accepted by God. He accepts us right where we are, sin and all.

The more parents can grasp this principle, the better their relationship with their children can be. A basic God-given need in every one of us is a *sense of security*—the idea that we are accepted, that we have worth. It is the bedrock of healthy self-esteem.

Nathaniel Branden, a psychologist who has written a great deal on self-image, has pointed out that man's need for self-esteem is inherent in his nature. But he is not born with the knowledge of what will satisfy that need or the standard by which self-esteem is to be gauged. He must discover it. Unfortunately, many approaches to meeting the need for self-esteem are self-destructive.

False Box Tops Won't Help Solve Life's Puzzle

Have you ever worked a jigsaw puzzle? The way most people begin is to spread out all the pieces and look at the box top to get an idea of how the picture goes together. By using the box top, you can start building the corners and the sides of the puzzle and then work in toward the middle. The picture on the box top gives you an idea of the puzzle's design—how it goes together.

In a very real sense, life is a puzzle, but people are trying to put that puzzle together with the wrong box top. It is as if somebody switched box tops on them and they are trying to relate to the pieces of life by using the wrong blueprint, so to speak.

As we work with groups of parents and young people, Josh and I identify at least four of life's false box tops: physical appearance, performance, position, and possessions.

I have yet to meet anyone who has not wrestled with some factor regarding his or her *physical appearance*. In his book, *Hide or Seek*, Dr. James Dobson includes a chapter on "The Gold Coin of Human Worth"—in other words, beauty.[1]

But no matter how hard we try and no matter how many billions of dollars we spend as a nation to be more attractive, we will continue to pursue that false box top if we are interested in discovering the key to human worth. In fact, putting undue emphasis on physical appearance can often lead to pursuing the second false box top—*performance*. Do you remember Dumbo, the little elephant with the giant ears? He was rejected because of his physical appearance, so what did he do? He compensated by learning how to fly.

There are many people who believe they can't make it on appearance so they compensate with performance. As we will see in the next chapter, it is important to appreciate the child's performance, but only after the child knows beyond a shadow of a doubt that performance has nothing to do with self-worth.

A "B" Had Him Ready to Commit Hara-kiri

A campus chaplain brought a college student to my counseling office because the young man was on the threshold of committing suicide. He was a pre-med student at a major university and he had received his first B in fourteen years of schooling. I could still recall that when I got my first B, I went out and celebrated. But this young man's first B had him talking about killing himself and he didn't seem to be bluffing.

He was the oldest son in a Japanese family and, if you know anything about Asian culture, you realize he was under tremendous pressure. His sense of self-worth was almost entirely based upon his performance, and now that he had "failed" by getting a B, his threats of suicide were to be taken very seriously, indeed. Fortunately, I was able to work with him and talk him out of it.

Possessions and Position Are Also False Goals

In addition to physical appearance and performance, there is the false box top of *possessions*. From infancy we are placed in front of a box with a screen on the front that brings the message of materialism daily, saying in a thousand different ways: "Buy! Purchase! Own!" In one study, researchers estimated that by the time a student graduates from high school, he has seen around three hundred and fifty thousand commercials.[2]

As Stephen Eyre points out in his excellent book, *Defeating the Dragons of the World,* the advertising experts tell us in dozens of ways that we can feel better about ourselves if only we own more. But we must buy the right car, the right home, the right clothes, and the right toothpaste. Only then will our problems be over.

Madison Avenue's siren song says anything is attainable— success, peace of mind, happiness—if only we will buy and own. The media blitz lures us " . . . to believe that our identity is tied up in what we possess. We come to think 'I am what I own.' We become what we have been labeled, 'Consumers.'"[3]

Along with possessions, we also pursue the false box top of *position.* We all seem to be born with the natural ability to play the game called "one-upmanship." Jesus spent three years trying to teach His disciples that their real concerns should not be with what they accumulate in worldly goods or how "high" they would rise on some kind of ladder of achievement. Instead, He kept talking about "laying up your treasures in heaven" (Matthew 6:19–21).

In Mark's Gospel, we come upon a scene where Jesus has been traveling with His disciples. After walking all day, they arrive at their destination and Jesus asks, "What were you arguing about on the road?"

Suddenly there is dead silence. None of the disciples wants to admit that he had been arguing about who was the greatest. So Jesus sits all of them down and says, "If anyone wants to be first, he must be the very last, the servant of all" (Mark 9:33–35).

With one incisive remark, Jesus lets His disciples know that they all have equal value. Their worth as human beings is not to be gauged on which of them is the "greatest." Instead, Jesus paints the picture of the servant who is secure enough to be willing to be last instead of first. Here is the epitome of true leadership and true greatness.

After giving them their lesson on servanthood, Jesus took a little child who was present and scooped him up in His arms, saying, "Whoever welcomes one of these little ones in My name welcomes Me; and whoever welcomes Me does not welcome Me but the One Who sent Me" (Mark 9:37, NIV).

Why did Jesus use the example of a small child to make His point? Because the disciples were arguing their worth, based on their accomplishments and their credentials, Jesus decided to turn to the one person present who had no credentials or track record.

What Jesus was saying was, "You must come to Me as a small child might come—without pretense, without guile. There is no need to show Me your works, your accomplishments—any reasons for Me and My Heavenly Father to love you. We love you as We love a small child who turns to Us in complete trust."

Your worth is not based on your accomplishments, credentials, or status. Your worth is not based on what you have or what you do. Your worth is based on *who you are,* a person created in the image of God.

Plumbing the Depths of "God Is Love"

To understand more fully what Jesus was telling His disciples (and us), we need to go back to the very essence of who God is. John, a disciple who needed Jesus' lesson about greatness as much as or more than anyone present, went on to a long career as an apostle. In addition to his Gospel, he wrote three letters to the Christian church. In one of those letters, he shared the simple but profound truth that "God is love" (1 John 4:17). The Greek word John used for love is *agape*—unconditional, totally self-giving love which has no desire or need for recompense.

It is clear, then, by definition, that God's very nature means that He needs to give. God's *agape* love must have an object—that is, someone to love. This may sound as if God created all of us in order to meet His own needs. If that is true, however, we are left with a dilemma, because then God would not be a self-sustaining God. The way out of that dilemma, is to realize that God could have nicely satisfied His need to love within the Trinity. He could totally satisfy His completely giving nature in the Godhead—the Father, the Son, and the Holy Spirit. God really didn't need anybody beyond Himself, but we find in Genesis that God said, "Let *Us* (the Father, the Son and the Holy Spirit) make man in *Our* image, both male and female" (see Genesis 1:26).

The point is, God did not *need* us; He *wanted* us, and still wants us. We are finite creatures made in the image of an infinite God. That means He has created us with the ability to enter into love relationships—with Him and with other people, particularly our children. But to enter into any meaningful relationship, two things are necessary: choice and trust.

God created us with the ability to choose—good or evil. The first man and woman miserably failed that test, and the rest of us have been paying the price ever since. Adam and Eve chose evil because they failed to trust God and what He had told them. But while the image of God in man was marred by original sin, it was not totally erased. God still loved man with unconditional love and sent His Son to the cross to prove it.

God Had More He Wanted Me to Learn

My years of private practice in family counseling convinced me that there was a real need to create a place where Christians could come to better understand the character of God and their own unique worth in His sight. Eventually I left private counseling practice and moved to Julian, a small rustic community in the mountains east of San Diego, California, to help found The Julian Center, a non-profit organization dedicated to helping people of all ages, in all walks of life, develop a Christian world view and understanding of their culture. To do this, we offered a course of study designed to integrate and use all facets of God's truth: biblical, psychological, historical, and scientific. Our goal was to influence and develop the *whole person*—intellectually, socially, personally, relationally, and spiritually.

Later, Josh and his family moved to Julian and he became a resident instructor on our faculty. For more than ten years we saw The Julian Center profoundly change the Christian walk of businessmen, housewives, seminary and graduate students, Christian workers, missionaries, and young believers alike.

Our curricula included studies in theology, philosophy, history, art, psychology, and sociology. During intensive twelve-week courses, we also focused on each student's relationships—with others and with himself.

A special feature was a "wilderness experience segment" that included rock climbing, backpacking, and survival tests, all aimed at improving the students' abilities to cope under stress.

All the theology I had learned in seminary and had developed into the specialized curriculum at The Julian Center focused on God's unconditional acceptance. I thought I had a fairly good grasp of this great truth, which I had discovered when I became a Christian in my late twenties. By then I was already married with four small children. After coming to Christ, I vowed to bring up my children according to God's highest ideal of unconditional acceptance. Charlotte and I had reared our first four children according to our understanding of this greatest of biblical principles. Nonetheless, years later, it became apparent that God felt I still had some lessons to learn.

How Theology Took On Flesh and Blood

Sixteen years after our fourth child was born, Jonathan came along when I was in my mid-forties. Jonathan was a very special little boy, a "preemie" who weighed under five pounds when he came into the world. Some people might say having a child in your forties is an accident, or at best, an "unplanned blessing." But I prefer to think that God sent Jonathan to us to let us experience rearing a child from birth as Christian parents.

After we brought Jonathan home from the hospital, I would walk into his bedroom every night, look down at him in his crib, and marvel that he was mine. It must have been the way Abraham felt when he had Isaac so late in life.

"Wow, he's mine," I'd say. "Look at that little guy. Look at that blonde hair. He's mine—thank You, God!"

I did that night after night, week after week, year after year for six years. In Jonathan, we had our little "crown prince."

When Jonathan was six years old, Charlotte and I had the privilege of going to Korea to take part in a great evangelistic campaign sponsored by Campus Crusade for Christ. The results of that campaign were absolutely phenomenal. On the closing night, in Yoido Plaza, 2.7 million Christians—the largest known gathering of Christians at one place at one time—came together to pray and praise God. To hear over two and a half million voices singing the "Hallelujah Chorus" brought tears to my eyes.

The impression made on me that night was tremendous, but it didn't really change my life. And yet my life was to be radically changed by that visit to Korea, just twenty-four hours before Charlotte and I were due to board the plane to come back to the United States.

The day before we were due to leave Korea, Charlotte and I found ourselves in an orphanage on the outskirts of Seoul on a rainy Sunday morning.

Why had we gone to that orphanage? I didn't need an heir. We didn't need any more children—we had five already. Four of them were boys, so I had plenty of people to carry on the Day family name. There were plenty of people available to divide up any meager inheritance I might leave behind.

No, we didn't need any more children, but we wanted to share our love and our family with a child who had neither. Finally, the director brought in five children and said, "Which one do you want?"

"Which one did we want?" It left us in the position of having to choose. Like a bucket of cold water in the face, we realized that we were looking for only one child, and the other four would have to remain behind. Because two of them were babes in arms, we knew they were not the ones God wanted for us. We didn't want to start a third family, we only wanted to expand our second family— that is, find a brother or sister for Jonathan. That narrowed our choices down to three: a little four-year-old girl, a five-year-old boy, and a six-year-old girl.

The little four-year-old girl hadn't been in the room for more than a minute when she climbed up on my lap and began to snuggle and talk her way into my heart. Meanwhile, the little six-year-old girl acted like a little mother. She pampered and took care of the little babies before they were taken away. She also seemed to be very precious, very special.

And then we turned to the little five-year-old boy who seemed rather indifferent to the whole process. Charlotte and I had to excuse ourselves and we stepped outside where we began to pray. Then we began to weep. We prayed some more. Then we wept and prayed, and wept again.

I thank God it was raining that day because I could step outside and let the rain splash on my face. Otherwise, I'm sure the director of the orphanage would have thought that Americans are emotional basket cases, and he might have decided not to let us have any of the children.

But as we prayed, God made it clear who it was that we should choose. And, as only God can do, He confirmed that choice in

Charlotte's heart and in mine without either of us knowing what the other had decided. We were both stumbling around, trying to guess the desires of the other.

Almost out of desperation, we devised our own method of "casting lots." At a given signal, each of us would put down a certain number of fingers in the palm of our other hand, indicating our choice. One finger meant the four-year-old, two fingers meant the five-year-old, and three fingers would mean the six-year-old.

Simultaneously, we both indicated our choice, and we were amazed to see that we had both put down two fingers. Although Charlotte had been thinking I wanted the four-year-old girl and I had been sure she wanted the six-year-old girl, when it came time to choose, the five-year-old boy was the one the Lord had put on both our hearts.

The director smiled, and then hurried away to prepare the adoption papers. With the choice over, I thought the rest would be easy, but then my real struggle began. The thought suddenly hit me, *Can I love this little boy as much as I love Jonathan—my "crown prince"?* And then I heard a still, small voice say, "Dick, what are you constantly telling people in your marriage and family counseling? Love is a choice. It's not how you feel about this—it's whether or not you want to choose to love."

I knew then that I would have to take a step of faith and make that choice. Actually, I needed to choose to make a *commitment* to this child—to love him for the rest of his life just as much as I loved Jonathan or any of my other children.

We signed the papers and the next day we left on the plane to fly back home. I kept running through my mind what had happened, and slowly an analogy took shape.

The "Crown Prince" and the "Chosen One"

We had our little "crown prince" in Jonathan, born to us late in life just as Isaac had been born to Abraham. And now we had our "chosen one"—little Timmy, as we had decided to call him. Then it all came together for me and the analogy made perfect sense. For the first time, perhaps, the theology that I thought I had learned so well in seminary took on the form of living flesh and blood. According to my theology, I knew that God is the Father, Jesus Christ is the Son (the "crown prince"), and that I, Dick Day, was the "chosen one." I did not choose God, He chose me. The same is true for any person who believes.

And what of my human, finite analogy? I took the part of the father, Jonathan was the "crown prince," and little Timmy was my "chosen one."

As I pondered all this, I got a new perspective of what acceptance is all about. God chose me and has loved me with an unconditional, everlasting love. I had chosen Timmy and committed myself to that very same kind of unconditional, everlasting love. Because I was secure in my knowledge of God's unconditional love for me, I could build that same kind of security in my children.

This book shares many wonderful truths and offers many invaluable and practical ideas for how to parent children. But absolutely basic to all that this book says is *the God-given worth of every child.* Christians sometimes make the mistake of thinking that they suddenly become worth something when they believe in Christ and become identified with Him. They think that up until that point, they have been worthless, depraved sinners headed for hell. Nothing could be further from the truth. Our worth is not in our identification with Christ, but our worth is secured—that is, it is made sure in our hearts and our minds—*through* our identification with Christ.

If that sounds like splitting theological hairs, think with me for a moment. If only Christians have worth, why should we care about starving Africans or unborn children? They are not identified with Christ. The answer has to be that, despite the fall of man into sin, every human being still has worth because he is made in the image of God. Yes, the image is horribly marred, stained, and warped, but the image and the worth are still there. Man's worth is rooted in God's creative plan, proven by His redemption and secured through salvation. God does not *need* us. Yet in His sovereignty He chooses to love us, not because He *needs* us, but because He *wants* us.

As parents made in the image of God, we are to portray that image as best as we possibly can to our children. Our first responsibility is to constantly make them aware that they, too, are made in the image of God—that they have ultimate value.

After Timmy arrived in America and became part of our home, he spent many months adjusting to us and our new culture. One day I asked him, "Timmy, would you ever like to go back to Korea?"

"Oh, no," he said.

"Why not?" I asked, curious about what he would say. I will never forget his answer: "Because here I am somebody special."

That pretty well says it, don't you think? We can put acceptance in theological terms. We can explain acceptance with psychological jargon, but the bottom line is being able to say, "Here—in my family—*I am somebody special.*"

May every child in your home be able to say the same.

To Think About, Discuss, or Try for Yourself

1.   In this chapter, Dick points out that children want to be accepted so badly that they will sometimes use unacceptable behavior to gain attention. What does this tell you about the critical need for acceptance in each of us?

2.   In this chapter, Dick lists four "false box tops" that people sometimes use to fill their need for acceptance and security: *physical appearance, performance, possessions,* and *position.* Which of these four box tops have been a problem for you and which might be proving to be a problem for your children? Talk with your spouse and decide if both of you are being positive or negative role models for your children in these four areas. What are your children picking up from your actions and lifestyle?

3.   This chapter closes with the story of Timmy, the Korean child adopted by Dick and Charlotte when Timmy was five years old. They knew that Timmy had become a real part of the family when he said that he would not want to go back to Korea because, "Here I am somebody special." Specifically, how do you make each of your children feel "I am somebody special"?

Part III

Appreciation:
The Key to
Feeling Significant

As we saw in Part II, acceptance is all-important, because first of all we want to know that our *being* matters. Following right on the heels of acceptance is appreciation—knowing that our *doing* matters also. It's not just a desire for praise, as important as praise can be. Appreciation has to do with *significance*—feeling that you have importance and that your accomplishments do make a difference to someone. That's why it's vital that parents appreciate what their children do, while always being careful not to put them on a performance basis. The next two chapters will talk about how to walk this fine line as you learn:

- why appreciation must be built upon acceptance
- how to appreciate your children without putting them on a performance basis
- why one out of three who live on a performance basis becomes a perfectionist
- the mistakes many parents make while believing they are doing the right thing
- the secret of putting appreciation to work in your home on a daily basis
- the signs of perfectionism and what to do about them
- how to model excellence instead of perfectionism
- the power of that little word *no*
- how competition can turn into a pursuit of perfectionism and a "winning is everything" mentality
- how to compete *with* instead of *against* and use competition to become the best you can be.

7

Catch Them Doing
Something Right

As our children grew from infancy into their early grade school years, I did my best to apply principles Dick Day had taught and modeled for me. I knew my kids needed unconditional love and acceptance, and I did my best to provide it every day. But I had one major problem—me.

Although coming to Christ while in college had done much to free me from a lack of self-worth, my early experience in Christian groups and churches had taught me that while God is loving, He is also very down on sin. If a Christian is to please God, he must hate sin as much as God does and live his life accordingly.

After I married Dottie and our children started arriving, I drew on my early Christian background and assumed that a parent's job is to keep his children from sinning. I told myself, *If I spare the rod and spoil my children, that won't be pleasing to God.*

It was not that I was abusive, but in those early years of parenting, I must have been what the kids call "a real drag." I was always quick to pounce on them if they made mistakes, but I didn't take enough time to praise them for what they did right. It seemed my main approach to parenting was to go around catching my children doing something wrong, or, at least, trying to stop them before they did something wrong. I thought I had an absolute obligation—no, a grave responsibility—to correct practically everything they did.

Quick to Criticize—Slow to Praise

My attitude was very evident in my actions. For example, let's say I was sitting in my study writing a book and I had a chapter really flowing, and then Dottie came in and said, "Honey, Sean just came home with all A's on his report card."

"Honey, that's great," I'd probably reply. "I'm right in the middle of a chapter. I'll talk to him about it at dinner."

At dinner I might remember to talk to him about it, and then, again, I might not. The point was, when Sean or any of the other children did something worthy of praise, I didn't necessarily jump on it in an instant to express my pride and appreciation.

But suppose Dottie had walked in and said, as she sometimes had to, "Honey, Sean just clobbered Katie for going into his room."

"He did *what*!? Send him in here right now. I want to *talk* to him!" News that my son had smacked his little sister got a totally different reaction. Suddenly, my chapter wasn't as important. The matter couldn't wait until dinner. I had to deal with it *now,* because I had to straighten out my son and be sure he was disciplined properly.

I could give you countless examples of the same syndrome with Kelly and Katie. (Remember, Heather wasn't on the scene yet.) What I didn't realize was that I was teaching my children something that I didn't want to communicate at all: "The fastest way to get Dad's attention is to do something *wrong.*"

Today as I talk to young people across the country, I estimate that fifteen out of twenty kids tell me that's exactly how it is at their house. They can get their parents' attention much faster if they do something wrong.

Recently, I was listening to a "Focus on the Family" broadcast. Dr. James Dobson's guests that day were four women, all of whom had become sexually involved in their teen-age years and now, in their early twenties, they were paying the emotional consequences. As I recall the broadcast, three out of the four made specific statements to the effect, "The fastest way to get my dad's attention was to do something wrong."

I don't know how long I would have gone on with my negative approach to parenting. It was simply too easy to catch my kids doing things wrong. Besides, it gave me a chance to be righteously autocratic. It made me believe I was "doing my job" as a parent.

The One-Minute Manager to the Rescue

Around 1984, when Kelly was ten, Sean was eight, and Katie was four, God spoke to me through a book. No, it wasn't the Bible. Instead, a friend told me about a slender little volume that had been on the market for a year or so—*The One-Minute Manager.*[1]

Written by Kenneth Blanchard and Spencer Johnson, *The One-Minute Manager* is a brief, fast-moving allegory that quickly and concisely spells out how a manager in any typical company or corporation can help his people set proper goals and then guide them in reaching those goals by giving frequent praise as well as effective reprimands. According to Blanchard and Johnson, the One-Minute Manager moves among his people, trying to "catch them doing something right." And when he does, he quickly shows them appreciation and encouragement for their efforts.

I didn't have to read very far to get the point. *The One-Minute Manager* is not a book on parenting, per se, but it was telling me something that I desperately needed to know as a parent. Instead of seeing my parenting job as primarily a matter of catching my kids doing something wrong and making sure to correct them, I learned to take a fresh look at how I was relating to my children. My new motto was:

"Try to catch your kids doing something right."

It's funny how one little phrase can bring a concept or principle to life. I was sold on giving my kids unconditional acceptance, but I had been struggling with learning how to appreciate them. It isn't that I never praised them for what they did; it was simply a matter of praising them *after* I was sure I had corrected all the things they had done wrong. Naturally, because kids have a tendency to make mistakes, it was just too easy to find them doing things wrong. Mix that with their intuitive ability to perceive that the best way to get my attention was to do something wrong and I had a real problem.

My Parental Schizophrenia Vanished

One side of me had been trying to accept my children, and the other side had been trying to correct them for doing things wrong.

It was no wonder that I often felt a little schizophrenic! But all that changed when I turned the emphasis upside down. Instead of concentrating on what they were doing *wrong,* I started to make a conscious effort to look for what they were doing *right.* My new goal was to find at least two things about each child that I could appreciate every day, and then be sure to compliment each child on what I saw.

I'm not sure my children noticed any "overnight difference," but I know I did. My whole perspective on parenting changed.

I would look over and see Kelly studying and then stop a moment to say, "Honey, I appreciate the way you study." When I saw Sean taking out the trash, I would stop him and say, "Sean, thanks for remembering to take the trash out."

I'd find little Katie picking up her toys, and I'd say, "Katie, sweetheart, Daddy really appreciates how you take care of your toys."

Another thing I began to do was try to find all of the children in the same general area—our family room for example—and stand in the middle of all of them for an "appreciation session." In this case, I wouldn't necessarily say anything out loud, but I would consciously stop for three minutes to ask myself, *How many things can you appreciate about your kids if you stop to think about it right now?* Then I would try to mentally list fifteen or twenty things I appreciated about the four of them. That meant finding about four or five items per child, but I always made it well within the three-minute time limit I set for myself.

This little exercise helped remind me of just how much I have to be thankful for about my kids, and it kept me primed for saying appreciative things at the proper time. You see, it isn't a matter of not being able to find things to appreciate about your kids; what it's all about is programming yourself to *speak up and tell your kids what you see*—to give them honest praise for their effort.

I talk to parents who have the concept of parenting I used to have, and they say: "Well, a kid is *supposed* to do certain things. Why should he be praised for something as ordinary as taking out the trash?"

My response is, "Why not? How do you feel when you are praised for doing your job?"

Anyone loves to hear the boss say, "I appreciate the way you handled that sale." Anyone loves to cook a good meal and have everyone in the family say, "That was *great*—you couldn't have fixed anything that would have tasted any better!"

Appreciation Is a Biblical Principle

As I've studied Scripture, I have found frequent examples of appreciation. When John the Baptist baptized Jesus, His Heavenly Father expressed appreciation by saying, "This is My Son, Whom I love, with Him I am well pleased" (Matthew 3:17, NIV).

If the Heavenly Father took time to express appreciation for His Son in front of the watching world, I can take time to appreciate my children at home or in public.

The apostle Paul always expressed appreciation toward the "spiritual children" he had begotten in churches he had started, and in several cases he singled out individuals for special encouragement. For example, Paul wrote to Timothy to tell him he constantly remembered him in his prayers and that he longed to see him because Timothy's sincere faith filled him with joy (2 Timothy 1:3–5).

If Paul could take time to appreciate his protégés, I can take time to appreciate my protégés—the children God has given me to train and nurture.

In a way, Paul was the original "one-minute manager." Although he had to play the role of disciplinarian, particularly with the Corinthian church, he made it a point to go around catching Christian believers doing something right, and he never hesitated to give them praise and encouragement.

We're All Still Learning

The key to the One-Minute Manager approach is to understand that we all like a sincere compliment. Unfortunately, a lot of people grow up not receiving nearly enough affirmation and praise. They eventually learn to become suspicious of compliments, thinking that perhaps they're being set up. I see this in my own family. Even today, after six or seven years of my new approach, my kids still don't always believe it. Sometimes it's fun to stop one of them and say, "Hey, I need to talk to you."

"Yeah, Dad. Is there something wrong?"

"No—I just want to tell you what a great job you did!"

And then I go on to spell out what that great job was.

Still, Kelly and Sean, in particular, may give me a bad time when I compliment them, saying something like "Ah, c'mon, Dad, what are you after *this* time?"

But I just smile and keep right on appreciating them—openly, enthusiastically, and even blatantly—because I know that they need it and I can tell they like it!

I guess we're all learning. I'm learning from my side and they're learning from theirs. But I have noticed that the more I catch them doing something right and praise them for it, the less I have to criticize and discipline them for doing something wrong. Praise becomes a motivator for proper behavior and, the plain fact is, I have to discipline them far less than I used to.

For example, I used to constantly criticize Kelly for throwing her clothes all over the room. I decided to begin going out of my way to try to catch her on occasions when she would put them in the clothes hamper and praise her for it. However, we're still a long way from calling this a victory, and although expressing appreciation often leads to the desired results, it doesn't always happen right away.

I used to admonish Heather not to squeeze her pet kitten so hard. I decided to start praising Heather for the times when she would treat the kitten gently. That worked, too, and I'm sure the kitten is particularly grateful!

Be Sure to Handle Appreciation with Care

Having said all this about appreciation, I need to put in a word of caution. Unless your children are absolutely sure you unconditionally accept them, praise and appreciation can become manipulative. A child will start to live on a performance basis, thinking, *If I do a good job . . . If I get A's . . . If I hit a home run . . . THEN my parents will appreciate me.*

Living life on a performance basis is what produces guilt feelings. I often ask groups of parents if they have ever felt guilty about failing at a task. Nearly every hand in the room goes up.

"Why?" I ask. "What does failing in a task have to do with morality?"

They get the point. When we fail at a task, we aren't really feeling guilt as much as we are feeling a sense of shame. And that sense of shame drives us into not being willing to accept ourselves, because we're really living life on a performance basis. That's exactly what happened to me as I grew up, always trying to perform, always trying to find the acceptance I never felt from my father.

That's why I bend over backwards to make my children feel accepted first, and *then* appreciated. For example, my two oldest children, Kelly and Sean, are fairly straight A students. When they get their report cards, I try to sit down with each one of them and talk about what they have achieved.

These talks have become something of a ritual in which I always assure them that, while I appreciate their earning good grades, I always want them to know: "Even if you didn't get A's, I would love you just as much and accept you just the same."

Recently, when I started giving Sean my speech, he beat me to the punch, saying, "I know, Dad. If I never got an A a day in my life you would love me just as much."

"That's right," I said.

And then Sean smiled and said with a twinkle in his eye, "But aren't you glad I got all A's?"

I had to admit Sean had me there, but I didn't mind. In Deuteronomy 10 the Lord God told the children of Israel He was giving them His commandments for their own good (v. 13). And that's how I want to parent my children—doing for them what is not easy for me, necessarily, but what is always for their own good and development.

"Yes," I told Sean. "I'm glad you got all A's because you are an A student. If you got C's and B's, I'd be upset and would take some creative steps to help you raise your grades. If you're capable of A's and I let you get away with C's and B's, I'm not doing the best I can for you."

In Katie's case, it's different. Dottie and I don't pressure her to make A's because she's more the B- and C+ student. How do we know the different abilities of our kids? We watch them, work with them, and encourage them. We always have a good idea of what they're working on in school and how they're coming along with it.

We also talk to their teachers. Dottie and I have always worked hard at having great relationships with our children's teachers. We have always appreciated their input and they have always appreciated our involvement. Our kids' teachers know we're interested and they know they can tell us the truth.

What I want Sean and Kelly to understand is that if I let them go through high school getting few or no A's at all, I'd be failing them and they would be paying the price for the rest of their lives. The same is true for Katie. If we let her slough off and not get the C+ and B- grades she's capable of, we would be failing her as well.

Give Them the Freedom to Achieve

Admittedly, there is a fine line to walk here. But the best way to walk that line is to *start with acceptance, then move to appreciation.* Make your children feel so secure, so loved, and so full of self-worth that they know they have the freedom to fail. Then they are much more likely to relax and achieve their full potential. Whether they're working for grades in school, participating in athletics, or engaging in any other endeavor, they're doing it out of feelings of self-worth, not performing in a desperate effort to be accepted. I always like to say this:

I appreciate my child's effort more than my child's accomplishment, and I appreciate my child's worth as a human being even more than my child's effort.

Sometimes I'm asked if appreciating the child's effort might still be a "condition" that would push the child toward living on a performance basis. That's certainly possible, but for me the best safeguard against that happening is to never stop working at accepting and then appreciating my children. No matter how long I'm at it, I'll never be a "natural" or an "expert." I will always have to work at being an acceptant, appreciative father.

I Still Fight the Old Nemesis

Old habits are hard to break, and if I let down my guard for even a moment, I'll be right back where I was, looking for what my kids do wrong instead of catching them doing things right. Trying to change is a lifetime job, and I fight the "God's wrath approach to parenting" to this day. Whenever my kids misbehave, my first and natural inclination is to crack down. No matter how I try, the old reaction, the old way of doing things, wells up within me.

Always, there are two barriers that I must overcome. One which I've already mentioned is past habits. If I do not concentrate on taking the time to accept and appreciate my kids, I won't do it. I know how valuable it is. I know how important it is, but if I don't have it in the forefront of my mind every day, I will let opportunities go by and soon I won't be doing it much at all.

The second barrier is that Satan really does prowl about like a roaring lion (1 Peter 5:8), and one of his most potent weapons is rationalization. I could easily tell myself, *My father was an alcoholic.*

He never spent time accepting and appreciating me and I turned out okay.

But that would only be an excuse to shirk my responsibilities as a parent Besides, my kids are growing up in a totally different culture from the one I knew. My kids face pressures that didn't even exist when I was their age. They need all the help they can get.

Because I never stop concentrating on accepting and appreciating my children, they know exactly what I mean when I urge them to "do your best." I'm trying to equip them to live in a very competitive world. As members of the human race, we're all in competition. In the next chapter, Dick will talk about positive and negative ways to compete and how to help your child pursue excellence instead of being trapped by perfectionism.

To Think About, Discuss, or Try for Yourself

1.   Is your approach to parenting primarily "catching them doing something wrong" or "catching them doing something right"? What would your children say?

2.   According to Josh's story, why was it easy for him to think that parenting meant correcting and criticizing first and praising later, if at all? Has the same thing ever happened to you?

3.   According to this chapter, why is praise so powerful? What does praise have to do with being a good parent?

4.   Why should parents use appreciation with care? What can happen if they don't lay plenty of groundwork for appreciation by assuring their children they accept them?

5.   Check the *One-Minute Manager* out of the library (or buy your own copy) and read it several times. Jot down ideas you get for better parenting.

6.   For additional biblical examples of expressing appreciation, see Romans 1:8, Ephesians 1:15–16, Colossians 1:3–4, 1 Thessalonians 1:2–3, 2 Thessalonians 2:3–4, Philemon 1:4–7. What central idea or thread seems to run through all of Paul's expressions of appreciation? What can you learn to help you express appreciation to your children?

7.   If you have not been making it a habit to openly express appreciation for what your children do right, start now by finding at least two things you can appreciate about each child every day. When you find something to appreciate, *be sure to tell your child,* no matter how awkward it may seem at first. It will get easier later.

8.   After becoming proficient in appreciation, try Josh's "appreciation session" idea sometime. The dinner table could be a good setting.

8

How Not to Grow
a Perfectionist
(*Dick Day*)

IN CHAPTER 7, Josh mentioned the danger in putting children on a performance basis. I'd like to pick up on that thought and focus on a particular problem I have seen over the years. This particular problem is called perfectionism, and it often surfaced when I was counseling children and adults who felt they had to perform well in order to be accepted.

Let's look at a typical example of perfectionism in a woman I'll call Barbara, who came to see me because her medical doctor could find nothing physically wrong with her even though she was continually tired and depressed. When she recited her schedule, I could understand why.

Barbara worked full-time in a boutique—because she enjoyed it, not because she needed the money. She was a mainstay in the parent-teacher organization, as well as a faithful member of the Sunday school staff of her church, where she had taught in the pre-school department for the past several years. She also sang in her church choir, and was available for Vacation Bible School every summer.

As we talked, I learned that she was very proud of her only child, Jennifer, who was a straight A student, star player on her junior-high volleyball team, and "absolutely no trouble at home." In fact, Jennifer often covered for Barbara, helping get dinner on, and doing much of the housework.

"I don't know what I'd do without Jennifer," sighed Barbara. "She's a remarkable kid. Jim and I are so proud of her."

"Tell me more about Jennifer," I invited.

For the next fifteen minutes, Barbara described Jennifer in glowing terms. Her daughter was a shoo-in for valedictorian of her eighth-grade class, and she was already planning to be valedictorian of her graduating high-school class as well.

"But she's not just a bookworm," Barbara assured me. "She loves sports and is really competitive. Her volleyball coach is sure she'll play varsity in high school. All she has to do is control her temper a little bit. She hates to miss a ball, and she can't stand it if her team loses."

"Where do you think she got the competitive streak?" I wondered aloud.

"Well, Jim and I always stress doing your best," Barbara replied. "I've always been pretty competitive myself—in fact, Jim says he dreads playing me in Scrabble because I always wipe him out."

"You mentioned Jennifer's temper—does it flare often?"

Barbara's face clouded a bit and she replied, "Well, to be honest, Jennifer does have a little problem. I try to get her to slow down, but she just keeps going at top speed. Besides her studies and sports, she's in three or four clubs and is president of one of them. And now she wants to start doing more babysitting to earn some extra money for clothes. She is a little short with me sometimes, but it's no wonder with all the pressure she puts on herself."

I could go on relating my session with Barbara, who is really a composite of many women I've counseled over the years. But I believe you see the problem. Unfortunately, it is obvious to just about everyone but Barbara. The telltale signs are there. Barbara is a perfectionist, and she is teaching her daughter to be one as well.

Both of them are living on a performance basis, and before I could ever help Barbara understand why she is so tired, I would have to get at why she pushes herself so hard. Then I would have to go on to help Barbara see that Jennifer is following in her footsteps. She is learning from her mother to always bite off a little more than she can chew. It's apparent that Jennifer's life is an "all or nothing" proposition. She must always get an A, she must always please her parents, and she must always win her volleyball games.

For Jennifer, winning is everything; finishing second is not enough, and getting a B is unthinkable. Jennifer is learning to compete against the world—and herself—every day of her life. She is following Mom down the fast lane of performance living.

The Subtle Power of Expectations

There are many subtle ways to put a child into the fast lane of performance living. One of the first things parents often do is place all kinds of expectations upon them. Sometimes parents want their children to accomplish something they didn't accomplish—for example, playing varsity football, becoming homecoming queen, getting a better job or a higher education. Parents often want to live out their lives through their children, and this places their kids under tremendous pressure to perform the way Mom and Dad expect them to. Add expectations at home to the expectations they find at school from teachers and peer groups, and the pressure can become fierce.

For kids growing up in Christian homes, the capper often comes from the church. I have talked to many Christian kids who grew up with the distinct impression that they had to be perfect. Because being perfect is not a realistic way to live, the only way they could pull it off was to wear a spiritual mask—particularly around adults. They were sometimes able to be honest with their friends, but with their parents, their Sunday school teachers, and their youth directors, they learned to "play the game."

It's ironic that we have so many people in churches today who are putting up a front of perfectionism when the Bible tells the same story over and over again of people who were not perfect—people who failed, sometimes miserably.

My wife, Charlotte, and I had the privilege of serving as counselors at the Billy Graham Association Congress for Itinerant Evangelists at Amsterdam, Holland, in 1983 and again in 1986. Tragically, we heard the same complaints again and again. Third World evangelists and pastors kept telling us, "We don't have anybody we can go to. We can't go to our mission boards, we can't go to our elders or other lay leaders, we can't go to our people because we're supposed to be the ones that they are looking up to. We have no one with whom we can share our problems."

If your children are very young, you may want to stop right now and think about the kinds of expectations you are placing upon them. Parents often pride themselves on expecting their children to do well. The old saying goes, "If you want a lot out of someone, expect it."

To challenge a child is one thing, but expecting too much starts the child on a vicious cycle, living on a performance basis. Some psychologists believe when people are put on a performance basis, one out of three becomes a perfectionist. Occasionally we will describe someone as a perfectionist in complimentary terms. The truth is, perfectionism is a terrible burden to carry through life. It can lead to mental disorders, procrastination, anorexia, bulimia—even suicide.

The Telltale Signs of Perfectionism

Perfectionists have an all-or-nothing mentality. They must be perfect—nothing less will do. This attitude often traps them into thinking there is nothing they can't accomplish. The word "no" doesn't seem to be in their vocabularies, and they usually bite off far more than they can chew.

Another typical characteristic of perfectionism is getting overwhelmed by the big picture. Having bitten off more than they can chew, and wanting to do it all perfectly with no mistakes or flaws whatsoever, perfectionists look down the track and see incredible obstacles. They wonder how they ever got into this and how will they ever get it all done? Or perhaps they won't even try, for fear of failure.

As perfectionists see all those hurdles ahead, they often draw back and procrastinate. A procrastinator is often a perfectionist who is putting off something because he feels he doesn't have time to do a really good job. Obviously, the longer a perfectionist procrastinates the worse it gets, but in the end he can always bail out saying, "If only I'd had more time—*then* I could have done something much more acceptable." But the real problem is the fear of failure and rejection.

And that brings up another characteristic—perfectionists find it hard to finish a project. They keep wanting to make it better. They are never satisfied.

As we could see in Barbara's daughter, Jennifer, perfectionists tend to get irritated when things go wrong. They are not patient with others or themselves. Perfectionists can't understand why other people don't have their high standards.

Perfectionists also "should" themselves a great deal, as in, "I *should* take care of that" or "I *shouldn't* say that."

Perfectionists tend to get down on themselves if they fail or make mistakes. Failure—any kind of failure—is unacceptable.

Perfectionists keep trying harder so they can "do better next time." This only spurs them into another round of all-or-nothing thinking, setting another group of impossible goals, and then feeling overwhelmed when they can't quite meet all of them.[1]

As we saw in Barbara's case, perfectionists can get burned out from trying to jump through too many hoops at once. They may want to draw back or drop out for awhile because they're afraid to fail.

Are Your Children Afraid to Fail?

Living on a performance basis makes many people afraid to fail. Are your children learning to take some risks in life, or are they learning it's better to play it safe?

A look at some typical "hero" types shows that they were all well-acquainted with failure:

- Thomas Edison failed thousands of times before he finally invented the light bulb.

- Babe Ruth, one of the great sports heros of all time, hit sixty home runs, a record that stood for decades before being broken by Roger Maris.[2] That same year, however, Ruth set another record—for strike outs.

- Abraham Lincoln failed politically and personally many times before finally becoming president of the United States.

Names like Albert Einstein, Winston Churchill, and Benjamin Franklin also bring images of heroes to our minds. Yet all of them, at one time or another, were fired from their jobs.

Something all heroes have in common is the willingness to take risks, to be different, even to fail in the pursuit of what they believe is worthwhile and right. What kind of example do you set for your own children, concerning wanting to be different? I'm not talking about moral issues, but being different by taking liberty to venture out, to learn, to find, to discover.

There is a real difference between allowing children freedom to fail and demanding that they strive for perfection, which only puts them in a double bind. On one hand, they learn to play it safe and not take any risks. They don't come up with anything very original. On the other hand, they strive for perfection in certain regimented and organized ways.

Everyone is going through a process called life. We are walking through that process, but we will never arrive, because life is a journey, not a destination. As we walk along, most of us are set on accomplishing something. We have goals. We are results-oriented.

Goals and goal-setting have become big business in recent years. Seminars and workshops are held by corporations across the country to help their employees set and reach goals.

What about your child's goals? What kind of goals does your child set because of your example, your guidance, your expectations?

It's good to have goals and it's good to want results, but if goals and results are reached at the expense of enjoying the process, then you have missed life. We all need to be enthusiastic about the process of life, and learn to pass our enthusiasm—not our extreme expectations—along to our children.

Teach Them to Compete With, Not Against

Part of communicating appreciation to your child involves the area of competition. According to child development specialist Erik Erikson, one of the stages through which every child goes begins when he "leaves home" to venture out into his school experience. As he goes into kindergarten and first grade, he enters the developmental stage called *industry*.[3] For the first time he runs smack into a competitive world, where what he produces becomes very important. Now is when parents need to become encouragers and affirmers, appreciating what the child does, but always basing their appreciation on accepting the child for who he is.

As the child moves into this industry stage, it's better to teach him that he is competing *with* people, not *against* them. Unfortunately, the typical school system is designed to teach children to compete against each other. So many get A's, so many get B's, so many get C's, and D's, and so many have to flunk. In sports, the child learns early that winning is what counts. It is no exaggeration to say that for children in the typical school experience, *competing against* is a way of life.

The trouble with competing against, however, it that it is always a win-lose situation. Whenever you play the win-lose game, you will eventually wind up a loser. You can't win them all. That means, in a sense, everybody out there in that competitive world is your enemy.

On the other hand, *competing with* is a different kind of game. Your opponent is not your enemy as much as he or she is your ally. He becomes someone who helps you maximize your own ability. Whoever crosses the finish line first is not that important. Competing to become the best you can be is what really matters.

I realize that the "competing with" philosophy sounds naive and that in the dog-eat-dog "real world" it is usually laughed at. Even so, there are many illustrations of people who "competed with" and became winners.

Why "Chariots of Fire" Was a Winner

The Academy Award-winning film "Chariots of Fire" depicts the stark contrast between "competing against" and "competing with" in the story of two gifted runners: Harold Abrahams, son of a Lithuanian Jew, and Eric Liddle, whose family was deeply involved in Christian missionary work. Both men won the honor of representing Great Britain in the 1924 Olympic Games in Paris, but their mental approach was much different.

Battling what he perceived to be the anti-Semitism held by his Cambridge University classmates, Harold Abrahams struggled to prove himself by competing against everyone in sight. He developed such a "winning is everything" attitude that he wound up hiring his own private track coach, with whom he trained in seclusion to prepare for the Olympic contest.

At one point, Abrahams articulated his "me against the world" philosophy by saying, "I don't run to take a beating; if I can't win, I won't run. I run to win."

Meanwhile, Eric Liddle also prepared for the games, facing the disappointment of his sister, Jenny, who believed her brother's running would lure him away from serving God. Liddle tried to explain that he fully intended to pursue a missionary career, but that he must first compete in the Paris games—not for his glory, but for God's.

"God made me fast," he told Jenny. "When I run, I feel His pleasure. To win is to honor Him."

Abrahams won a gold medal in the 100-meter dash, while Liddle refused to compete in that race because his qualifying heat was run on Sunday. For Liddle, that meant violating his strong conviction that the Sabbath should be kept holy. A teammate gave up his spot in the 400-meter competition and let Liddle run in his place. Liddle won a gold medal in that event.

When the games were over, however, Abrahams seemed to feel little joy in his accomplishment. We get a clue concerning why he could not savor his victory from remarks that he made before the race. At one point he said, "I'm forever in pursuit and don't even know what it is I'm chasing." Just before the race, in his dressing room, he admitted, "I've known the fear of losing. Now I'm almost too frightened to win."

Eric Liddle, on the other hand, enjoyed his victory. When asked by a teammate how he felt about dropping out of the 100- meter dash to honor his firm belief in keeping the Sabbath holy, he said, "I have regrets, but no doubts."

Liddle went on to a long missionary career in China, often running the back roads or riding his bicycle for miles for the sheer joy of it. In the 1940s he was imprisoned by occupying Japanese forces, and he died in a prison camp just before the end of World War II.

In life, Eric Liddle competed *with* instead of *against*. His epitaph could have easily been what someone said of him during the glory days of his Olympic triumph: "He ran in God's Name, and the world stood back in wonder."

When parents can communicate to their children that what counts is doing their best, they help free them from the win-lose mentality. They help their children catch the subtle but very real difference between competing *with* instead of competing *against*. That's why it is so important to appreciate your children's effort more than their win/lose record. When your children know that they are more important than any result on a scoreboard or a grade sheet, then they can relax, feeling secure and free to give it their best shot, knowing that they can excel or fail and it won't make any difference as far as your acceptance is concerned.

Our Volleyball "Champs" Never Won a Match

Last year Julian High School, two hundred students strong, participated with other schools in volleyball for the first time. They got off to a less-than-auspicious start with "walk on" coaches and a patched-together schedule that left them with one home match and the rest on the road, playing against much larger schools with more experienced players.

Our teen-age sons, Jonathan and Timmy, were on the team, and Charlotte and I joined a number of other parents who never missed a match. We traveled up and down the mountain yelling our heads off while our 1–A level kids lost match after match to stronger 3–A level opponents.

By season's end they had not won a single match. They had won some games, but a match is three out of five, and they never quite managed to pull off a victory.

But that did not matter to us. We cheered Jonathan and Timmy as though they were world-class, because in our minds they are. Their record didn't matter. They gave it all they had. They never complained or bad-mouthed anyone and they never hung their heads in shame. We cheered them on as if they were champions, something we have always done since both boys were small.

Every certificate, every award or recognition they received went up on the hallway wall outside their bedrooms. It didn't matter what it was—good citizenship, an art award, a ribbon won at a track meet—every single one went up there to affirm Jonathan and Timmy as human beings. We have always affirmed what they do, while being sure to affirm who they are. That hallway wall became a statement by Mom and Dad that said, "We're proud of you and what you've done."

As you may recall, Timothy and Jonathan are our "second family," having arrived more than fifteen years after our first four children. But with our older children, we tried to do the same kind of affirming. Dick, Dave, and Jeff were outstanding distance runners in high school and college, and my office looked like an athletic trophy room because every top shelf of my bookcases was lined with awards. When people walked into my office, they knew I was proud of my kids' achievements. But what a casual visitor might not have understood was that I was much prouder of my boys as human beings. They didn't have to run the performance treadmill, having to perform and win in order to get my acceptance. I might add that my only daughter, Kimmy, is a trophy herself. She is Dad's only "little princess," even though she is a mature and beautiful "daughter of the king" and mother of three (see Proverbs 31:29).

I also worked very hard at having them know the difference between sibling rivalry and sibling jealousy. Sibling rivalry is natural.

I believe it's the basis for competing with one another. But sibling jealousy leads to competing against. One child tries to put the other down to make himself look better. Children can get into playing the game of "I'm okay, you're not okay," and that is competition at its worst.

One of our concerns when we adopted Timmy was how Jonathan might respond to him. Our next youngest, Jeff, was sixteen years older than Jonathan, who was in many ways like an only child since his older brothers and sister had already left home. He was the "crown prince," and we worried that he might be jealous of anyone invading his "turf." But our worries were unfounded.

Yes, there is some sibling rivalry between Jonathan and Timmy, but not jealousy. Charlotte and I strongly believe that this is due to the influence of two role models, their brothers Dave and Jeff. I know of no two men who have been more accepting and encouraging of each other. Although they competed in the same sports, they were prime examples of *competing with* rather than *competing against*.

Jonathan and Timmy also had the "legend" of their older brother, Dick, who was already living and working in Africa. God used him to put together an entire famine-relief program for Mali, one of the most stricken nations in Africa.

In areas where God gifted our children I always urged that they strive for excellence, but not perfectionism. When you pursue excellence—doing the best you can to become the best you can be—you can "lose" and still come out a winner. I don't agree with Vince Lombardi. In fact, I am quite sure that *winning is not everything!*

He Set a World Record and Came in Second

A few years ago, Steve Scott, a premier American miler, competed in a big international invitational meet in San Diego. Steve broke the record in the indoor mile that night, but he still came in second, because Emin Coghlan ran even faster. Afterward, a reporter interviewed Steve and asked him the inevitable question: "How do you feel after giving such a great performance and coming in second?"

I will never forget Steve's answer. As I recall his words, he said: "I accomplished the goal that I had set, but Emin had a higher goal and he accomplished his. Still, I accomplished my goal and I'm satisfied."

Steve Scott didn't like losing to Emin Coghlan, but he could still go away satisfied because he knew that he had maximized what he could do. Yes, he would have liked to have finished first and had the world record, but he didn't have to apologize to anybody for what he had done because he had given it his all.

Steve Scott's attitude is another example of competing with instead of against. Whenever possible, take off the pressure and let your child know that he does not have to compete against. Teach your child to compete with, to be cooperative, and to be compassionate. I believe the greatest accomplishment in life is the building of character, and a key part of character is learning compassion for others. No matter how brilliant or accomplished someone is, if that person has not learned compassion for other people, his or her life is a failure. Remember:

You can't be compassionate when you are going for the jugular.

Along with all this, I want my children to understand that they need to have compassion for themselves. The perfectionist can't have compassion for himself. He drives himself toward higher and higher goals, never content with what he does because it is never enough. The perfectionist cannot accept himself.

That's why appreciating a child must always be done within the framework of your acceptance of that child. Only when a child feels accepted can he become an autonomous, trusting individual, free to make his own decisions, free to accept appreciation for what it is— a sign of your love and affirmation, not some kind of payment for being "good enough."

When Timmy Finally Felt Accepted

In chapter 6, I related the story of how we adopted our son Timmy from a Korean orphanage when he was five. When Timmy arrived in the United States and became part of our family, he immediately went on a "performance basis." He couldn't do enough to please. He was obedient to the gnat's eyelash. Even though Timmy couldn't speak English and we couldn't speak Korean, we could tell that he wanted to please us—to perform.

At first, I explained his behavior by thinking that's what he learned in his own culture, particularly the Oriental tradition of obedience to adults. But after a few weeks, it became very evident what Timmy's real motivation was. An international student conference was being held at The Julian Center where I was director, and I learned that a Korean girl would be there.

What an opportunity, I thought. *Here's somebody Timmy can talk to. He's been here four weeks and had no communication with anyone in his own language.*

I took Timmy over to the conference center and found the Korean girl. She was a lovely, friendly person with a big smile, but when she said something to Timmy in Korean, he turned on his heel, grabbed me by the legs, and clung to me trembling. I picked him up and hugged him, and he grabbed me by my beard saying over and over, "Dadda, Dadda, Dadda. . . ."

I apologized to the Korean girl, telling her that I had no idea what was wrong and that it certainly wasn't her fault. Later I figured it out. When I took Timmy to meet a Korean girl and she spoke to him in Korean, his five-year-old logic told him: *They want to send me back . . . I'm going to have to go back to Korea.*

Not long afterward, Charlotte, Timmy, and I went up to San Francisco for a weekend visit. We went down to Fisherman's Wharf and Timmy had a great time. Then we decided it would be fun to take the cable car and go up to Chinatown. Again, I thought, *Timmy would love some Oriental food and being in a place that would remind him of Korea.*

And again I was wrong. When we got to Chinatown, Timmy just clammed up. We went to a couple of stores and did a little shopping and then ate in a restaurant, but the entire time he never said a word. Finally, we left, got back on the cable car, and rode back down to Fisherman's Wharf. Suddenly, as if by magic, Timmy brightened up, and was happy the rest of the day.

Later, when Charlotte and I talked about it, we decided that it wasn't as much a matter of "They are going to send me back to Korea" as it had been a reminder of some of his hurt. Also, there was the longing to identify with us and always to please us. This went on for several more weeks, and then we had the day that I call "the turning point."

We were at breakfast and I asked Timmy to do something. I'm not quite sure what it was anymore. Something perhaps as innocuous as "Hurry and finish your breakfast, Timmy, you have to get ready for school."

But instead of jumping to obey me as he usually did, Timmy hesitated. There wasn't open rebellion on his face, but there was a look that said, "I'll have to think about that."

I looked at Charlotte to see if she had caught the significance of Timmy's response. Her eyes told me that she had. Timmy had made one giant step toward becoming an autonomous person who could make his own decisions. With that small act of "defiance," Timmy let us know that he was secure enough in our home that now, when asked to do something he could obey us, not because he was making some robot-like response out of fear, but because he knew that we loved him and he could decide for himself to obey.

Since then, Timmy has totally identified with our family. In fact, he taught me a great lesson in what identification really is. While studying the American Revolution in the fifth grade, Timmy raised his hand and told the teacher that he had a great-, great-, great-grandfather who had signed the Declaration of Independence. When I tell this story, most people chuckle because they don't believe any Orientals signed the Declaration of Independence. Yet Timmy had grasped a truth that many Christians still don't understand. He was identifying himself with the Day family of past, present, and future generations through his adoption, just as we are identified with Christ, past, present, and future, by our own adoption into the kingdom of God.

The Person Always Comes First

In accepting and then appreciating your child, it comes down to what I call the primary and the secondary. The person is always primary, his performance is always secondary. First, you deal with the child's *being*—the acceptance which gives the child security and self-worth. Then, you deal with the child's *doing*—the appreciation which makes the child feel significant. Whenever you express appreciation for what the child *does,* it should always come out of your acceptance of who the child *is*.

Today, Timmy is sixteen and you may be wondering how he came out. He is not perfect. He has his problems, and sometimes he needs discipline just as any normal teen-ager does. But it's interesting to note that he is a phenomenal helper around our home. He loves to cook. He washes dishes. He helps because he *wants to,* not because he has to. That warms my heart because I know Timmy isn't performing in order to be accepted. He *knows* he's accepted, and out of that he responds freely, knowing he has the freedom to fail and certain we appreciate him for who he is, not what he does.

To Think About, Discuss, or Try for Yourself

1.   What kind of expectations did your parents place on you as a child? What kind of expectations are you placing on your children?

2.   Is perfectionism a problem for you or any of your children? Review the "telltale signs of perfectionism" on page 98. Do you see any of these in your own life or in your child's? For example, do you "should" yourself a lot? If any members of your family show signs of perfectionistic behavior, try to point these out to each other and encourage each other to change.

3.   Talk with your spouse and honestly ask yourselves, "Are we doing anything to put our children on a performance basis?" That is, do your children feel they have to perform in order to gain your acceptance? Or do your children know without a doubt that you accept them no matter how they perform? If you are not sure, try talking to your children to learn their true feelings.

4.   Do your children have the freedom to fail? What would they say if they felt they could be honest?

5.   Why is "competing with" better than "competing against"? Is Dick's approach to competition practical? How can you help your child learn to compete with others with the goal of becoming the best he or she can be?

6.   Which answer best describes your family? For us, winning is:
      a. Everything
      b. Unimportant
      c. A worthwhile goal

7.   This chapter asserts: "You can't be compassionate when you are going for the jugular." Do you agree or disagree? Talk with your spouse about what it takes to be a compassionate person.

Part IV

Affection:
Without It Children
Can Perish

IF YOUR acceptance and appreciation of your children are to come alive, they must receive ample—even overflowing—amounts of your affection. To a child, parental affection is like water to a plant, oil to an engine, food to the starving. With no affection an infant can literally die. Without adequate affection, a child can grow into a teenager who is willing to trade sex for feeling loved. The next two chapters explain in detail why affection is so powerful, including:

- why kids want and need hugs so desperately
- why hugs and kisses can make children healthier
- how parents mistakenly give less affection as children grow older and why they should give more
- why teenagers need affection from parents now more than ever
- the tremendous sexual pressure on teenagers from their peers and the media
- the main reason why teens are sexually active
- why we need to learn how to love
- why the love of parents for one another is the greatest builder of security for a child
- tips for husbands on how to let your children know "I really love your mom"
- why tasteful sex is okay for heroes
- tips from other parents on how to show your kids affection.

9

The Awesome Power of the Simple Hug

It HAD been a very long speaking tour and I found myself in Phoenix, Arizona, a town I sometimes describe as: "no water, but a lot of beach." It was late spring and temperatures were already starting to climb past the ninety-degree mark. I had several high schools to cover that week, and one day I found it necessary to do an assembly outdoors at noon on the school lawn. This particular high school had an enrollment of about one thousand and it seemed as if almost every one of the kids had come out to sit on the grass and listen to some guy talk to them about sex.

I was that guy. Standing on a boulder to be seen and heard a little better, I began speaking on why so many young people trade sex in their search for true love and intimacy. Just as I got going, a group of punkers walked up and joined the crowd.

Their dyed hair was combed in all kinds of typically weird arrangements, and gold chains hung from their necks. Their arrival didn't cause much commotion, but I kept my eyes on them as I talked, unsure of why they were there or what they might do. But they just stood there, looking at me as if to say,

"We dare you to say anything that we would want to listen to, McDowell."

Twenty-two minutes later, I finished spelling out my thoughts on the difference between real love and the cheap substitute so many kids think they have to settle for in the back seat of a car. As I stepped down off the boulder, the leader of the punker group ran right up to me!

There, before the entire school assembly of almost a thousand kids, this husky young guy came within inches of my nose, so most of the crowd didn't really see or hear what happened next. They couldn't see the tears running down his cheeks or hear him ask me a poignant question:

"Mr. McDowell, would you give me a hug?"

Before I could even get my hands up to put my arms around him, the big punker grabbed me in a bear hug, put his head on my shoulder, and started crying like a baby. I hugged him back and we stood there like that for what seemed to be over a minute. Just about any hug might seem long when it's from a big husky punker whose gold chains are imbedded in your chest. But I could see the kid was sincere. He wasn't putting me or the crowd on. He really wanted a hug!

Finally, the punker stepped back and said something that has become a typical statement from many teens: "Mr. McDowell, my father has never once ever hugged me or told me he loved me."

In his own dramatic style, this young man in the weird garb, the crazy hairdo, and the gold chains made a statement about the universal need for affection that I believe many in that crowd of nearly one thousand high school kids never forgot. And I also believe that this young guy's poignant words about his dad make an important statement to all parents about the importance of touching, stroking, hugging, and kissing your children at every opportunity.

Children Can Die without Affection

You're probably familiar with the statistics about the need young children have for affection. For example, one research study done around the turn of the century showed how infants who were not hugged and kissed sometimes actually died from lack of affection. There have been a lot of other experiments and research studies in recent years. These studies show that when somebody cares about you, cherishes you, and treats you with tenderness, it literally makes you healthier. But children who are not treated with affection do not develop properly, even though they may be well-nourished otherwise.

Throughout the world, one of the first needs infants communicate is the desire to be cuddled, hugged, and stroked. Affection makes children happy, but even more importantly, affection meets a basic physical and psychological need that doesn't really change that much as children grow older.

As I mentioned in chapter 2, one study revealed that parents tend to hug and kiss children when they are younger, but the hugging and kissing become less frequent as they grow older. By the time children hit junior high and high school, many parents practically stop hugging and kissing them altogether. One reason for this is that teen-agers brush their parents away, saying that they are "grown up now and don't need it." Don't believe them! They *do* need affection, and if they don't get it, they will fulfill their need in the wrong way.

Children are arriving at puberty—sexual maturity—earlier with practically every decade. A hundred years ago the average age for puberty was sixteen. In the 1950s puberty was occurring at an average age of fourteen. Today, as the twentieth century moves toward its close, the average age for the onset of puberty is closer to twelve.

I don't give you these statistics as interesting trivia, but as something very important to think about. Puberty means a lot more than menstrual periods and nocturnal emissions. Puberty means that a child enters into adulthood as far as ability to "make babies" is concerned. Unfortunately, because children are entering puberty at younger ages than ever, they are even less capable of handling the tremendous emotional stress involved in undergoing the bodily changes related to adolescence.

The High Cost of the "New Morality"

Everyone has heard of the "new morality," a term that came out of the sexual revolution that has supposedly occurred in the last several decades. Actually, the new morality is nothing more than the old immorality gone to seed. The bombardment of sexually suggestive television shows, films, videos, books, and magazine articles for teen-agers is incredible.

During one year of average television viewing, a child ten or older will be exposed to more than nine thousand scenes suggesting sexual intercourse, or making sexual comments, or sexual innuendos. Out of these nine thousand scenes, more than seven thousand—about 80 percent—portray sex outside of marriage. By the time a teen-ager turns twenty, he or she has seen and heard ninety thousand sexual comments and suggested sex acts on television.[1]

Is it really any wonder that more and more teen-agers are engaging in pre-marital sex? In one Vermont high school, a health education teacher gave a confidential survey to incoming ninth graders. The results showed that more than 50 percent of them had already engaged in sexual intercourse. The survey also revealed that 80 percent of the students polled had their first sexual experience "spontaneously," and more than 90 percent said they didn't use contraceptives in their first encounter.[2] And this was in *Vermont*—not exactly the fastest track in the nation, socially speaking.

In another survey, a New York polling firm canvased thirteen hundred students in sixteen high schools throughout the United States, plus sixteen hundred students in ten colleges, and five hundred parents of teen-agers in twelve cities. They did not poll impoverished inter-cities or rural areas, striving instead to discover the opinions on sex of supposedly mainstream, typical suburban adolescents. This poll showed:

- students who had lost their virginity: high school, 57 percent; college, 79 percent
- average age at which teen-agers first have sex: 16.9
- teen-agers who engage in sex from once a month to once a week: high school, 33 percent; college, 52 percent
- sexually active teen-agers who know AIDS can be spread heterosexually: high school, 96 percent; college, 99 percent
- those who say AIDS has caused them to change their sexual behavior: high school, 26 percent; college, 15 percent.

Welcome to the World of AIDS

The onset of AIDS has supposedly caused many in our society to think twice about having premarital or extra-marital sex. But the horror stories continue to unfold. I received a letter from a friend who wrote:

Please, Josh, keep telling kids the reality that is facing them. My wife and I have a college-age friend whose life has been devastated.

Last fall she went to Florida to vacation for three weeks. While she was there she met a "wonderful" man. He treated her like royalty. She moved out of her hotel to spend the rest of her vacation living with him. She "fell in love."

At the end of the vacation he put her on a plane and gave her a *ring box*. He told her not to open it until she arrived back home. Like any red blooded "in love" woman with a ring box in her hand, she opened it as soon as the plane left the ground. When she opened the box, inside was a miniature coffin and a note that read, "Welcome to the world of AIDS." Three months after her return she tested HIV positive.

Josh, my understanding is that there is a warrant out for his arrest, because he is known to have done this same thing with at least seven other women.

This is criminal . . . but not telling them (kids) about the reality is just as criminal.

Teens Are Sexually Active by Default

I could go on with many other graphic accounts and startling statistics that came out of our "Why Wait?" research study of high school and college students in the late 1980s. After interviewing thousands of young people, Dick and I are convinced that many teen-agers and young singles are sexually active not because they really want to be, but because they don't have any deep personal reasons for waiting until they are married to have sexual intercourse.

Teen-agers do, however, have at least two deep personal reasons for getting involved in premarital sex. Whether I talk in a junior high, at a high school assembly, or at a university, I preface almost every talk by pointing out: "Almost every single one of you has two fears. One is the fear that you'll never be loved, and the other is the fear you will never be able to love."

Almost always there is absolute silence. Whenever I do assemblies for youth, I know I had better not make statements that are off, even by 5 percent. If I do, they'll shove that 5 percent right back down my throat. But I've never been challenged on listing these two fears. Deep down the kids know that I'm right. And it is these two fears that drive them into trading sex for intimacy.

When Dick and I were doing the *Why Wait?* book, the first section dealt with why young people are becoming sexually involved today.[3] We put all the data from our survey into the computer and, after it kicked out the answer, my manager walked in and said, "You won't believe this. The survey came out with thirty-seven documented reasons why kids become sexually involved today."

"That's depressing," I told him. "I hate to have to report that. Besides, I'm not sure a lot of people would even believe it. Maybe we can narrow it down."

I took the list and poured over it again and again, trying to see where I might scratch off ten or twelve of the thirty-seven reasons. I discovered I couldn't honestly remove one of them. So, I got a group of high school kids together and said, "Look, I need your help. Here is a list of thirty-seven reasons why kids say they become sexually involved. Are all of these legitimate, or can we get rid of some of them?"

This group of high school kids went over the list. They studied it for a long time, and they couldn't remove any of the reasons either! Granted, some of the reasons reveal narrow thinking, but they are all still legitimate opinions given by the teen-agers themselves on why they have premarital sex.

The list of thirty-seven reasons that we worked with ranged from the physical ("It's the natural thing to do," "It provides a thrill and releases tension") to the psychological ("It's a way to be popular," "I owed it to him," "I was curious"). There were also what we called "environmental" reasons (a lack of information about sex, broken homes, alcohol, and drugs).

Under emotional reasons was the one I've already mentioned—"the need to love and be loved." Another big one was "I was lonely." According to researcher John C. Woodward, who has studied lonely people for twenty years, high school girls are the loneliest people in the United States.[4]

Every Daughter Will Always Be "Daddy's Girl"

If high school girls are the loneliest people in our country, it's no wonder that another key reason I've often heard teen-agers give for engaging in premarital sex is that they are "in search of my father's love."

In his best-selling book *Always Daddy's Girl,* author and counselor H. Norman Wright says to all women:

Whether he was close or distant, present or absent, cold or warm, loving or abusive, your father has left his mark on you.

And your father is still influencing your life today—probably more than you realize.[5]

The truth of Norman Wright's words is substantiated in one of the most poignant letters I ever received, which came from a young woman who wrote:

When I was only fourteen years of age I dated an eighteen-year-old boy. After a month or so of dating, he told me that he loved me and that he had to have me. He said if I loved him I would have sex with him, and if I wouldn't he couldn't control his desire for me and we would have to break up.

What did I think at fourteen years of age? I knew sex was wrong before marriage, yet I so desired to have a man love me. I was so unsure of my father's love. I always felt as if I had to earn his love, that the better I was at home with the chores, the more my father would love me, the more A's on my report card, the more my father would love me. So here was my boyfriend, whom I really liked and thought I loved, telling me he loved me.

Well, I needed that love. And if the conditions to keep that love were to have sex with him, I felt I had no choice. I didn't want to lose my virginity, but also didn't want to lose the man who loved me, so I finally gave in.

Then, this girl went on to share something very private and intimate. In her letter she quoted an entry in her diary, dated August 11:

I felt lonely tonight and I thought about the many times in my life that I have felt lonely—intense loneliness as though I were in life all alone. And I realized that what I was lonely for was a daddy, to be able to call him up when I hurt and hear him say he understands and have him listen to me. And I could call him up because of our special relationship as I grew up. But I never had that with my dad, and so I am lonely without a link to my past.

And then I thought about the young girl who this very night will lose her virginity because she is searching for love, her daddy's love. And I wanted to be able to stop her somehow and tell her she'll never find it in another man. How my heart hurts when I think of this girl, when I think of myself so many years ago. My life has been one big search for my daddy's love.

At the age of fourteen, this girl let her eighteen-year-old boyfriend have his way. After two years, she broke up with him, but soon had another man and went through the same cycle with him. Then it was another, and another, and another. She admits in her letter that none of her relationships helped her find security. On the contrary, she was a puppet in any man's hands because she wanted desperately to find someone who would love her unconditionally.

She finally found that unconditional love at the age of twenty-one when she met Jesus Christ. She discovered that Christ loved her while she was still a sinner, that He died on the Cross for her sins so that she could be His child, and He could be her Father. At the age of twenty-one, after years of mistakes, heartache and pain, she had found the "Daddy" who would love her.

This young girl's story is one of countless examples. A mother came to me during a parent conference, showed me a picture of her beautiful fifteen-year-old daughter, and poured out her story to me:

> This year my daughter has had sex with seventeen men. A month ago she had an abortion and two weeks ago she attempted suicide. This morning she was leaving for school and I asked her, "Honey, why do you do it? Why are you doing this to yourself? Do you have such a sex drive or something you can't control it? What is it?"
>
> My daughter answered, "Mommy, I don't even think I have a sex drive. I don't even like sex."
>
> "Well, why are you doing it then?"
>
> "Mommy, at least when each guy gets through he tells me he loves me."

Recently a fourteen-year-old girl came up to me and said that during the previous week she had had sex with three different guys. I'm not sure what she thought I would do. Perhaps she was trying to shock me, but all I said was, "Why do you do it?"

Her answer: "Because at least for a moment I feel like I'm loved."

Teen-agers Struggle to Find Identity

It would be easy to just shake our fingers at teen-agers and deplore their "lack of moral conviction." But that really won't help. We have to go a lot deeper to get at the root cause of the problem. One reason I have bothered to share all these stories and letters with you is to focus on every parent's responsibility to display adequate amounts of affection in order to build the child's foundational needs of security and significance. When parents are consistently warm and affectionate toward their children, the children feel accepted and appreciated. And when you have felt that affection as a young child, you are less likely to sell out everything as a teen-ager because you want somebody to "love you."

When children reach teen-age years, they begin coping in earnest with another stage of development that psychologist Erik Erikson calls *identity*.[6] In other words, they are trying to put together everything that has gone before. They are wondering, "Who am I, really? Mom wants me to be a student, Dad wants me to be a jock. But what do *I* want to be? And does anyone care anyway?"

It is during these teen-age years that problems with self-image and self-esteem can hit with tremendous impact. As teen-agers seek for identity, they often try to meet their needs through their senses. According to one psychologist, the number one peak experience of life is sex and the number two peak experience involves music. And where are we today in much of the teen-age world regarding sex and music? From what I've seen and heard in my travels, it's somewhere in the suburbs of Sodom and Gomorrah!

Lacking solid footing in the stage of development called *identity*, it is no wonder that many teen-agers wander into all kinds of sexual mistakes. According to Erik Erikson's eight stages of development, your capacity for *intimacy* comes out of your *identity*.[7] Intimacy involves developing the capacity to invite another person or persons inside your very being, to be able to reveal yourself completely with all your weaknesses, fears, and doubts. But, if you don't know who you are (identity), it is virtually impossible to achieve true intimacy with someone else.

It's Easier to Bare Your Bottom Than Your Soul

But secular society—the originator of the new morality—has the answer. It offers a cheap imitation of "intimacy" in the form of sex, and many teen-agers (as well as many adults) buy into it. After all, if you have never established your true identity, it is much easier to bare your bottom in bed than to bare your soul to another human being and take that other person into the very depths of your life. As my co-author Dick Day puts it:

**"Intimacy happens when two people come together
and each is able to take the other into his or her life
completely, with no reservations, no pretense, no masks."**

Unfortunately, many people aren't capable of true intimacy because, lacking acceptance by key persons such as their parents, they have never learned to accept themselves. There is then no logical reason why they should assume that anyone else could accept them either, and as a result they hide. They wear a mask of sorts and never let people see behind that mask.

When teaching classes at The Julian Center, Dick has often opened sessions on intimacy by wearing a blank mask with absolutely no features on it. Students get the point almost immediately. When you wear a mask, others never know who you really are. And as long as you aren't willing to reveal who you truly are, you cannot achieve true intimacy with others.

The Best Reason for Teen-Agers to Wait

Earlier, I mentioned that our *Why Wait?* survey revealed thirty-seven reasons why teen-agers felt there was no reason to wait to have premarital sex. In another section of the *Why Wait?* book, we discussed twenty-six reasons why the teen-ager *should* wait. Obviously, we went over all the physical reasons: the fear of sexually transmitted diseases, particularly AIDS; the fear of unwanted pregnancy; the temptation to have an abortion.

We also touched on many good emotional reasons, for example, the psychological distress of guilt, possible destruction of self-esteem, the danger of being put on a performance basis. Debora Phillips, author of *Sexual Confidence* and director of the Princeton Center Behavior Therapy in New Jersey, has said:

> Due to the instant sex of the sexual revolution, people perform rather than make love. Many women can't achieve a sense of intimacy and their anxiety about how well they perform blocks their chances for honest arousal. Without genuine involvement, they haven't much chance for courtship, romance, or love. They're left feeling cheated and burned out.[8]

Obviously, the most telling reason for teen-agers to avoid premarital sex is that God says in His Word that it is wrong, dangerous, and even deadly. Scripture tells us that our bodies are the temple of the Holy Spirit and to use them immorally is to sin against ourselves (see 1 Corinthians 6:19).

And in another place, God's Word clearly says that it is His will that we should be holy, that we should avoid sexual immorality by learning to control our bodies in a way that is honorable. We should never try to take advantage of a brother (or a sister) to pursue passionate lust (see 1 Thessalonians 4:3–6).

Parents often make the mistake of emphasizing these "rules" that the Bible clearly states about sex. The rules are there, true, and they make good sense, but in order to communicate rules you need to build relationships. And the relationships you build with your children when they are young will deeply influence the relationships they have later.

If you give your kids enough affection, acceptance, and affirmation, they will be much more apt to understand why God has designed sex to be enjoyed within marriage.

I believe that through positive teaching and role-modeling, parents can help their children see the beauty of true intimacy in which people come together sexually, not because they want to use each other, but because they love each other. If children do not learn the true meaning of affection, love, and intimacy at home from their parents, *where will they learn it?*

Is Love Spoken at Your House?

I believe that two of Jesus' deepest teachings concerning love can be found in the Gospel of John, and both of these statements apply in a special way to the family.

In His parable of the vine and the branches, Jesus says, "As the Father loved me, I also have loved you; abide in My love" (John 15:9, NKJV). One place all of us abide is in our homes where we live with our families. What better setting could there be for "abiding in His love" than the home? Where would it be more necessary to abide in His love than in your family?

In His high priestly prayer on the night before He went to the cross, Jesus prayed that His disciples could be one, as He and the Father were one. And He went on to say, "May they be brought to complete unity to let the world know that You sent Me and have loved them even as You have loved Me" (John 17:23, NIV).

Every Christian home has the tremendous opportunity and challenge to model to the world the unity they know because they are loved by Jesus Christ. Because of His great love, they love one another. There is no more important truth to teach your children daily than this.

This chapter has only one message: Be sure to give your children huge daily doses of affection. Their very destiny, their very ability to some day function as effective and fulfilled wives, husbands, and parents depends on it.

You have probably seen the bumper sticker that asks, "Have You Hugged Your Kids Today?" That phrase is now so familiar that it has inspired all kinds of spin offs such as "Have You Hugged Your Dog . . . Your Horse . . . Your Gerbil?" I believe a far more important question is:

"How *Often* Have You Hugged Your Kids Today?"

You can't hug your kids enough, you really can't. And it doesn't really matter how old or what size they are. No one ever outgrows the need for affection. There is awesome power in a simple thing like a hug, a wink, and lips just forming the words "Hey, I love you!"

To be a hero, hug your kids and hug them often!

To Think About, Discuss, or Try for Yourself

1.   According to this chapter, what can happen to infants if they don't get enough affection? List what can happen to children who grow up with limited affection, particularly young girls who don't get enough affection from their fathers.

2.   According to this chapter, what are two deep personal reasons teen-agers get involved in premarital sex? What are teen-agers really seeking when they get involved in premarital sex?

3.   What is the secret to getting your children to obey the "biblical rules" concerning sex?

4.   Finish this sentence in a paragraph of twenty-five or thirty words: "There is awesome power in the simple hugs I give my children because . . ."

5.   Print your own "bumper sticker" on a sheet of paper and put it where you can see it every morning and every night:

"How Often Have You Hugged Your Kids Today?"

6.   God says in Jeremiah 31:1, "I have loved you with an everlasting love, with tender kindness I have drawn you." If this is how our heavenly Father draws us to Himself as His children, can you see how important it is for us as earthly parents to use the same approach with our own children?

10

The Greatest Thing You Can Do for Your Child

IT WAS the Valentine's Day broadcast on "Good Morning, America" several years ago and David Hartman was interviewing Dr. Benjamin Salk, a family psychologist. Because love was the obvious topic for the day, Hartman led off by asking, "Is everyone born with the capacity to love?"

"Yes," Dr. Salk answered.

"Then why don't we have more love in the world?" Hartman wanted to know.

"David," Dr. Salk wisely responded, "even though we are born with the capacity to love, we need to learn *how* to love."

And then Dr. Salk turned to the camera, looked right in the eyes of millions of people, and added: "The greatest thing you parents can do for your children is to love each other."

We agree! Dr. Salk put the problem and its solution in a nutshell. Everyone is born with the capacity to love, but everyone does not learn how to love unless he or she sees it modeled by the most important people in life—which usually means the parents.

There is no question that one of the greatest builders of security in a child is the love his parents have for him. But, I believe an equally great builder of security in the lives of children is the love their parents have for each other. A generation or two ago, most children felt secure about their parents' love for each other. But today that is not the case.

Unfortunately, many children are seeing precisely the opposite being modeled in their families and in the families of their friends. Husbands and wives do not demonstrate love toward one another. In today's culture, divorce is an easy out for too many people. And even if they manage to stay together, there is no warm intimacy or expression of love between them.

After talking to thousands of kids all over the country, I know that one of their greatest fears is that Dad is going to divorce Mom or vice versa. Every time I return from a speaking tour I am reinforced in the knowledge that one of the greatest heritages I can leave my children is my love for their mother.

How to Have a Happy Family

The sixth chapter of Ephesians opens with Paul admonishing children to obey their parents, to honor Mom and Dad. Then Paul singles out fathers in particular and adds, "Do not exasperate your children; instead, bring them up in the training and instruction of the Lord" (v. 4, NIV).

In Ephesians 6:1–4, we find a capsule description of how to have a happy family. Children are to obey, and parents—fathers especially—are to nurture the children wisely, lovingly, and fairly. But look back for a moment to Ephesians chapter 5. What is the context for the children obeying parents and fathers parenting children lovingly and wisely?

Husbands are to love their wives as Christ loved the church (v. 25). They are to love their wives just as much as they love their own bodies. "He who loves his wife loves himself" (v. 28, NIV). In addition, wives are to respect their husbands and follow their loving leadership (vs. 22–24, 33). The entire context of Paul's admonition to children to obey parents is built upon the supposition that the children have a father who loves their mother and a mother who loves their father.

When Kelly was younger, I used to say to her, "Kelly, do you know that I love your mother?" She would smile a little and reply, "Yeah, I know it."

"How do you know?"

"Because you always tell her."

"What if I lost my voice and couldn't tell her? How would you know then?"

"Because you always kiss her."

"What if I got chapped lips and couldn't kiss her? Then how would you know?"

Then Kelly would give me the answer I was looking for: "Because of the way you treat her."

That's always the acid test. How do I treat my wife? I can say I love her. I can give her a peck on the cheek as I rush out the door; but how I treat her as my children are watching every moment will tell the real story.

To those children, my actions speak louder than my words in showing their mother my love for her. My kids are not oblivious to the incongruity of my walk and my talk. Remember, you can con a con, you can fool a fool, but you can't kid a kid!

How Can I Tell Mom, "I Love You"?

One thing I have been doing for several years now involves including my children in my plans to get their mother special gifts— on anniversaries, for example (when I remember them!). I get the kids together and say, "I'm so lucky to be married to your mother, I just thank God that He led me to her. You know, kids, it's almost like a dream and I'm afraid that someday I'm going to wake up and find out it isn't true. Now, our anniversary is coming up and I need your help. What can I do to tell Mom, 'I love you, thanks for being my wife?'"

"You could take her to the beach because she loves the beach," Kelly ventured.

"Okay, I'll take her up to Laguna Beach to our favorite hotel," I replied.

"You could take her out for swordfish because Mom loves swordfish," added Katie.

"Great idea!" I said and picked up the phone. In front of the kids, I called our special restaurant in Laguna Beach and said, "Could you have a special swordfish dinner set off in a nice table in a corner and could you have a special 'You are loved' plate ready for my wife?"

All the while my kids were right there listening, watching, and knowing that I really do love their mom very much.

Not to be outdone with ideas for where to eat, Sean added, "For another meal you could take her out for spaghetti. She loves spaghetti, too."

"Another good idea!" I told Sean. And immediately, I dialed Salerno's Restaurant in Laguna Beach and made those arrangements for the second night.

Love Dots Can Pop Up Anywhere

I have also enjoyed including my children in planning gifts for Dottie's birthday and her Christmas presents, but beyond those big occasions, I keep looking for ways to tell Dottie I love her on the ordinary run-of-the-mill days as well.

"What can I do?" I ask the children. "Have you heard her say anything that I might be able to do to show her I love her?"

My kids just come alive to questions like that. One idea they gave me on Valentine's Day a few years ago was to go down to the Hallmark store and ask for some love coupons and love stickers. Ever since, on Valentine's Day, I have tried to make it a point to lay in a year's supply of these stickers, which I keep in my dresser drawer. Every so often throughout the year, on no particular special occasion, I'll pull out some stickers and start leaving them around where Dottie can find them. One might pop up on her cologne bottle, another on her bathrobe or her pillow. Each sticker (I like to call them "love dots") has a brief message, such as: "This gives you one trip to the opera," or "This is good for one dinner out at the restaurant of your choice this week."

My kids love this—especially when I go to the refrigerator and put a love dot on the milk, or on the butter. Then, when their mother comes in, they say, "Mom, why don't you look in the frig?"

Dottie smiles because she has heard this before and has a pretty good guess about why they want her to look in the refrigerator for something besides food for them. And then she'll pull out the love dot sticker and get my latest message that tells her I love her. But the kids are getting a message, too. They are hearing their father say to their mother, "I *love* you. I love *you*. I'm *committed* to you." Nothing—absolutely nothing—is a better builder of their security than that.

I Reach Out to Touch Them—Often

Because I'm on the road a lot I have one big phone bill. I call home practically every night and naturally I want to talk to everyone. One of the kids usually answers and after talking to Katie, for example,

I will say, "Honey, it's good talking to you, but, hey, is that fantastic mother of yours at home? Is that good-looking woman I'm married to there? Would you let her know her hubby is on the phone?"

There I will be—five thousand miles away in England, or stuck in an airport in Texas. But with the help of AT&T I reach out to touch my family and say to my children, "I'm committed to your mother." Every time I call I am consciously aware of reinforcing this principle:

My children's greatest security comes from knowing that I love their mother.

And after I ask for Dottie, the child who answered the phone will holler, "Mom, it's my fantastic dad!"

My kids are getting so used to this that they don't always need my prompting. One night I called home and talked to Sean for awhile. He was all excited about helping his basketball team win a game the night before. And then out of the blue he said, "Dad, do you want to talk to my fantastic mom?"

That tickled me because it tells me they are getting it. They are understanding that I really do believe I am married to the most fantastic woman on this earth.

Something else I do while on the road is send a gift home to my wife, but I'll send it in care of one of the children and say, "Please give this to your mom. Slip it to her as a special surprise."

Last week while in San Francisco with my eleven-year-old, Katie, I went to a large baseball souvenir shop and bought all kinds of memorabilia from the Boston Red Sox display and a team jacket for Dottie. She is an avid, no, an *ardent* Red Sox fan. Before wrapping the gifts I showed them to Katie. With childlike excitement, I told her how much I love her mom and why I bought these gifts for her. Then I had Katie take them home and give them to Dottie, saying, "These are from Daddy. He loves you."

Why do I bother with all this? Because I want to include my kids in the *specific* things I do to show their mother I love her. That way they don't have to guess; they *know* I love their mom because they've been in on a lot of the things I do to show her that love.

You Can't Talk to My Wife That Way!

I even show my love for Dottie in the way I discipline the children. Several years ago, before our oldest daughter had moved into the teens, she and Dottie got into a period of "my mother/ myself" tension. They just kind of grated on each other. Today it's just the other way around and they get along beautifully, but back when Kelly was about eleven, she began sassing Dottie and talking back to her in general.

After observing this a few times, I decided that enough was enough. I grabbed Kelly by the shoulders, gently swung her around, looked her in the eye and said, "Young lady, you might talk to your mother that way, but I will never let you talk to my wife that way! I love that woman, and I will not only protect her from people outside the family, but I will also protect her from you kids. Don't ever talk to my wife that way again!"

Kelly blinked, mumbled something, and walked away. But the results of my brief speech about how I wanted people to talk to my wife were unbelievable. It helped break Kelly of her habit of sassing Dottie back. A few times she would start to make some smart remark, catch herself, and look over at me and say, "Oh, I can't talk to your wife that way, can I?"

"No, Kelly, you can't," I'd reply with a twinkle in my eye. Even in disciplining your children you can reinforce the idea that "I am committed to my mate."

Something else I've done with the children is to read Proverbs 31:28–31, which talks about a husband praising his wife and the children praising their mother. I've done this with Dottie present and then we all discuss and think of things we can thank and praise Mom for. This little exercise accomplishes two things. First, the children have to think of something specific and positive to say about their mother, rather than just taking her for granted. For that matter, so do I. And second, the children hear me praising their mother and again they see that I am committed to her—my wife.

Sex Is Okay for Heroes, Too

Dick and I believe that one the most effective ways to build security in our children is to be openly, yet tastefully, affectionate toward our wives in front of our kids. We think it's very healthy for Mom and Dad to show physical affection to one another and to let the children know that sex is beautiful within the commitment of marriage.

Many parents are so reserved or embarrassed that they sometimes give their children the idea that sex is dirty—at least it's "something we don't talk about much around our house." There are many ways, however, to let your kids know that sex is part of your affection for one another within the commitment of marriage. And when children feel secure within the commitment that you and your wife have for each other, they sometimes come up with interesting observations.

Dick recalls the time Charlotte had been back in the Midwest speaking to a women's conference at Wheaten College. She had been gone about a week and was coming into San Diego on a six o'clock flight. As he prepared to drive from Julian down to San Diego—about sixty miles—he said to Timmy and Jonathan, then in their early teens, "Guys, would it be okay if you'd spend the night here by yourselves? Your older brother is just down the street and you can call him if you have a problem. I'd just kind of like to pick up Mom and spend the night down in San Diego at a hotel."

Timmy looked at his dad then got a big grin on his face. He gave Dick a gentle nudge in the ribs and with eyes sparkling he said, "Go for it, Dad! Go for it!"

It was obvious to Dick that Timmy was well aware of the birds and the bees and what Mom and Dad would be doing in the hotel that night. But Dick could also see that Timmy was not being disrespectful or suggestive. He was simply reflecting the attitude he had seen modeled before him by his parents concerning sex.* His remark had a sexual connotation, but it was a healthy one because Dick's children have been taught that sex is beautiful—something to be looked forward to within the context of marriage.

Each family will have to determine how they want to handle subject of sex. Every husband and wife will have to decide what is tasteful and what is not. But, every couple should make specific efforts to let their children know that sex is a very beautiful expression of affection between a husband and wife. As you are affectionate toward your children, don't fail to be affectionate toward each other in front of them. Their security will grow by leaps and bounds.

And How Do You Love *Your* Kids?

Showing affection to each other creates an all-important atmosphere in which your children can feel secure. Then you need

---

* For specific ideas see, *How To Help Your Child Say "No" to Sexual Pressure* (Word Books, 1987), chapter 6, "How to Model a Context for Sex," and chapter 10, "How To Teach Sex."

to follow through with those all-important hugs and kisses that make them feel special and lovable.

While Dick Day and I were making the video series "How to Be a Hero to Your Kids," we talked with several couples on camera to learn what they did to show affection to their children. One woman said, "I try daily to express love to my daughters. I hug them everyday. I have one who especially likes cuddling up, and she'll come and get in bed with me and we'll hug."

This girl is eleven, but she still loves her mother's hugs. Sometimes when her mom won't let her go she'll say, "Oh Mom, come on. . . ." But then Mom hugs her even more and she loves it. She also tells her mother, "You're my best friend."

In those same on-camera interviews, we talked to a father who said, "I think the best thing that I can do with my kids is get down on their level, where I can look them in the eye. It is so important to spend time together on the floor playing their games, with me involved in what they're doing—their toys, their ideas of fun, wrestling with them. I need to spend even more time reading books to them while they sit on my lap. And I also hug with them, cry with them, and ask them for their forgiveness when I've been unfair or impatient."

This man's wife added that he shows affection to her in front of the children as well. She commented that her little daughter had just told her, "Mom, you know when I get married and I'm pregnant my husband can kiss me, too."

Another couple with four daughters helped us zero in on how important it is for girls to receive plenty of affection from their fathers as they grow up. Dick asked Carrie, the mother, if her father had showed her much affection when she was a little girl, and she admitted he had not. Fortunately, she had an affectionate mom and other relatives who filled much of her need for hugging and touching, but she still missed getting it from Dad.

Now that Carrie is a mother of four little girls, she has mixed feelings when she sees her husband, Rick, a pediatrician, hugging and kissing them every day. One side of her is happy because her husband is fulfilling such an important need in the lives of their children, but she admits to a twinge of regret, because it reminds her of the affection she didn't get from her own father.

When I asked Rick how it feels when he hugs and kisses his four girls and tells them he loves them, he said: "It's one of the best feelings I could ever have in my life."

"Do you feel fulfilled as a dad?"

"I really do," said Rick. "When our oldest daughter was born, I was a little hesitant about showing affection, but with Carrie's urging, I've really gotten into it. There is no greater feeling than that."

Another way to teach your children about love among the family—and God's love—is through what Rolf Garborg calls "the family blessing."[1] In his excellent book by that same title, he shows how families can grow together and form a strong bond as parents teach their children about God, shape character development, and instill in them a sense of security and self-confidence by pronouncing a blessing (such as Numbers 6:24–26) over the children. By turning this family blessing into a nightly ritual, you can establish an excellent "spiritual" way of showing your children affection.

We All Need Our Daily Quota of Strokes

Dick Day refers to it as "the power of touch at the emotive level." Remember the research studies I mentioned concerning infants dying if they don't get cuddled and held? In a sense, we all die a little each day without hugs, pats, kisses, kind words—what psychologists informally call "strokes."

It's the way God designed us, and it starts at birth when a child naturally searches for its mother's breast. Mom can't prop her breasts, but she can prop a bottle, and when she does that vital contact is missing. We can't emphasize it too much: *Affection is a life-long need.*

We only wish parents like Carrie and Rick could be multiplied by the thousands across the land. Affectionate, physically demonstrative families could do more to help kids "Just Say No" to drugs than all the education programs combined, helpful as these programs are.

Neither one of us came from particularly affectionate, physically demonstrative families, but we're both making sure that our own families get plenty of cuddling and affection. A favorite pastime for Dick and Charlotte and their kids—even today with many of them fully grown—is just piling in bed together to hug, watch television, eat popcorn—whatever. Dick often says he's waiting for the bed to just collapse with a *"kathunk"*! But if that happens, he won't mind. The price of one bed would be well worth the affection his family shares.

Maybe piling in bed together is not your scene, but if you choose to try it, you're in good company. A photo by official White

House photographer David Valdez was released not long ago showing President Bush and his wife Barbara in bed with all their grandchildren.

Some parents, especially dads, may get concerned about just how affectionate they should be, particularly with daughters who are beginning to develop physically. This is a valid concern, but don't let it stop you from being affectionate in appropriate ways that are comfortable for you and your child. Choose your own approach to affection and then show it daily—in fact, several times a day.

Pssst! Hey! I Love You!

I know that openly showing our kids affection gives me tremendous feelings of fulfillment as a father and as a man. One of the things I like to do with my children is find them busy with homework, for example, and I'll stop what I'm doing for a moment and whisper loudly, "Pssst!" They're used to it now and they never respond to it the first time, because they know what's coming.

I keep saying, "Pssst," several times, and then they start to smile and sometimes even laugh. Then they manage to put on a straight face and they'll look over at me and say, "Yeah, Dad, whadda ya want now?"

That's when I wink at them and, while never saying the words out loud, I form "Hey! I love you!" with my lips.

It never fails. They can be in a bad mood, they may have had a really bad day at school, but every time they'll break out in a smile. And then they form the same words back to me: "I love you, too!"

Then I just go on with what I was doing—watching television, reading the paper, making a phone call. And they go back to their homework. You know, it doesn't take a lot of time to express that kind of affection, but it pays tremendous dividends. That's what lets them know that they are accepted and appreciated. That's what makes them feel secure and significant.

Whatever you do, don't be hampered by thinking that showing affection has to be "dignified" or "proper." For the past year and a half, my little four-year-old daughter, Heather, and I have been going through a special ritual when I call home while out on the road. It begins with us singing together over the telephone:

I love you a bushel and a peck,
A bushel and a peck,
And I love you all to . . .

And on the other end of the line, Heather yells at the top of her lungs, *"Heck*!"

Then I cap it off with silly noises that can't really be described on paper, but no matter, Heather loves it. And if I forget to add the noises she'll say, "Daddy, do it."

"Do what?"

"You know—*the noises.*"

With a little kid, you don't need to be fancy; any old crazy "love noise" will do.

Something else Heather and I do is get in arguments about who loves whom the most.

"I love you more than you love me."

"Well, I love you more than the whole world," counters Heather.

At this point, it would seem that Heather has won, but then I'll remind her of some basic astronomy lessons I've given her and say, "Well, I love you more than the whole *universe.*"

Even at the age of four, Heather understands that the universe is much bigger than the world, and she capitulates saying: "Wow, Daddy, there's no bigger love than that!"

I realize this doesn't sound like a very deep conversation, but in one sense I think it's pretty profound. Everytime it takes place it reminds a little four-year-old that there's nothing bigger than her daddy's love for her. That's worth the whole universe—and then some!

To Think About, Discuss, or Try for Yourself

1.   In this chapter, Josh maintains that one of the greatest builders of security in the lives of children is the love their parents have for each other (see Ephesians 5:25–28). If possible, discuss with your spouse how effectively you are displaying love toward one another before your children. Do they know that their parents love one another and that their home is secure? How can you and your spouse communicate this more effectively?

2.   *For dads only:* Have you ever tried including your children in plans to tell their mother how much you love her? Do any of the ideas Josh shares in this chapter seem applicable to your own family? If so, pick one out and try it soon.

3.   How is the subject of sex handled in your family? Do you and your spouse make any efforts to let your children know that sex is the ultimate expression of affection?

4.   On a scale of 1 to 10, with 10 meaning that you are very affectionate and give your children hugs, kisses, and other displays of affection, constantly, how would you rate yourself? How would you rate your spouse? If your spouse is relatively unaffectionate, discuss some specific things that can be done to increase displays of affection.

5.   *More for dads only:* Are you reticent about showing affection to your children, particularly your daughter because she's starting to mature and you fear that touching her in any way will be inappropriate or even incestual? If so, talk these fears over with your wife and discuss together how you can show affection to your daughter in ways that are comfortable for everyone.

Part V

Availability:
Making Time to Be
a Hero

IN THESE days of being overcommitted and overly busy, it's common to feel guilty about not spending enough time with the family. We hope the next two chapters help you get past "the guilties" to discover practical help and gain deeper understanding of the real issues involved in being available to your kids:

- why a two-year-old's needs are more important than a deadline
- how one father decided to change his ways and what it has meant to his family
- what being available—even when it's inconvenient—says to your child about his importance
- why availability is the key to positive parenting
- why today's parents are spending less time with their children and the choice they must make
- why there are no shortcuts to spending "quality time" with your kids
- why the consistent small moments are more important than the "big moments"
- how to get on your teen-ager's schedule
- how to get on your small child's agenda
- how to avoid the saddest words a parent could ever say
- how "early to bed, early to rise" makes one father a real hero
- dozens of specific ways to "hone in" on your children
- the fine art of asking questions—key to communicating with your kids
- why being a hero to their friends is so important
- keep a record of their lives—to preserve those priceless memories.

11

Love Is Spelled T-I-M-E

A LITTLE over thirteen years ago, I learned something about time management from my two-and-a-half-year-old son, Sean, and my wife, Dottie. The lesson they taught me is permanently engraved on my mind, and it happened while I was in my study, busily engaged in one of several projects that I usually have going at once. In this case I was right in the middle of a chapter for a new book when in wandered Sean.

"Want to play, Daddy," he chirped expectantly.

As an "experienced" parent (we had already been through the two-year-old stage with Kelly) I should have realized that basically, Sean just wanted a hug, a pat, and a minute or two to show me the new ball he was carrying. But I was working on an important chapter and I felt that I just didn't have even two minutes right then.

"Son, how about a little later? I'm right in the middle of a chapter."

Sean didn't know what a "chapter" was, but he got the message. Daddy was busy and he'd have to leave now. He trotted off without complaining and I returned to my manuscript. But my relief was short-lived. In a minute or two Dottie came in and sat down for a "little chat." My wife never tries to nail me; she has much gentler— and more effective—methods.

"Honey, Sean just told me you were too busy to play with him. I know that this book is important, but I'd like to point something out."

"What is that?" I asked a bit impatiently because now my wife was keeping me from my all-important project.

"Honey, I think you have to realize that you are always going to have contracts and you are always going to have deadlines. Your whole life you will be writing and doing other projects, but you're not always going to have a two-year-old son who wants to sit on your lap and ask you questions and show you his new ball."

"Honey, I think I hear what you're saying and you make a lot of sense as usual. But right now I've got to get through with this chapter."

"All right, Josh, but please think about it. You know, if we spend time with our kids now, they'll spend time with us later."

A Child Is Two Only Once

I did think about it. And the more I thought the more Dottie's gentle words were like a knife slicing into the core. She was right. I'd always have deadlines. There would always be contracts to fulfill, phone calls to answer, people to see, trips to take. But my boy would be two only once, and soon that year would be gone and then he'd be three, and four, and five—and would I have any more time for him *then*?

I knew what the answer would be if I didn't change my ways. Quietly, without any big speeches or fanfare, I made my decision. Ever since, I have tried to place my children ahead of contracts, deadlines, and the clamor of a world that wants me to get back "ASAP." Since then I have had an understanding with publishers that my family and my children must come first. If not, I would have to be constantly telling my child that "a book is more important than you are."

As I learned with my own two-year-old, you can't schedule a small child the way you schedule a committee meeting, or a doctor's appointment. The attention span of a small child is very, very short. And when you are willing to be available according to the child's agenda, you give the child permission to have that short attention span.

Often a child will want to play a game or whatever, but after a few minutes he wants to do something else. He may wander off to play with his own toys or see if it's time for Sesame Street.

I sometimes talk to parents who get frustrated, because their young children don't want to "finish what we start." I try to help them understand that it's okay to leave a game unfinished or to leave play undone. Play isn't something you finish, it's something you and your child enjoy..

Yes, all this takes patience. In our seminars, Dick Day often likes to point out that we parents just can't wait for our children to do certain things because we get impatient. We jump in and finish their prayer for them, or we take the hammer or saw away saying, "Here, let me help you."

The chief hallmark of being able to enter into a child's agenda is patience. We must be able to wait them out, hear them out, let them try it themselves, and if they don't quite get it right or don't finish it, we don't worry about it.

I believe it was John Wesley who said, "If you don't know how to teach children, then get children's tracts and read them until you know how to teach children."

All John Wesley was saying is that if you want to deal with a child, you must learn how the child thinks and be able to get on the child's wave length. Then you can start to see life through his eyes, according to his agenda, and that's when you will start to communicate.

Teen-Agers Need "Unscheduled" Time, Too

Fortunately, the lesson I learned when Sean was two has stuck with me over the years. Just recently, I was in the middle of writing a children's book in our favorite vacation retreat down in Mexico, right on the coast of Baja. One morning I was "on a roll" with the ideas really flowing when Kelly, my sixteen-year-old, walked in and said, "Daddy, would you take me to get my nails done?"

My first thought was, *Man, this is the last thing I needed right now.*

My second thought was, *Josh, practice what you preach about being available.*

My third thought was, *Lord, give me a joyful spirit.*

You see, I could have looked glum and said impatiently, "Okay I'll go." But then I might as well have given her the money for a cab and sent her on by herself.

Instead I said, "Honey, I'll be glad to. I'll be right with you."

I folded up my chapter, hoping that later I could "catch the roll" I had been on, and with joy I took my daughter to get her nails done. It wasn't just a matter of being her personal taxi driver to get her somewhere. What she really wanted was time with me, and we did have a good talk on the way down and back.

Kelly has thanked me at least three or four times since that day. Why? Because what I did said to her, "Honey, you are of such tremendous worth to me that I'm willing to interrupt what I'm doing, no matter how important it might be, and spend some time with you."

That's what acceptance and appreciation are really all about! They just aren't buzz words to throw around when you are trying to sound like a profound parent. Acceptance and appreciation tell the child that he or she is of tremendous worth. And I can only express my acceptance and appreciation through being affection-ate—*and available.*

Availability Says "You Are Truly Important"

When we're available to our children it says, "You are important." And when we're not available it says, "Oh, yes, I love you, but other things still come ahead of you. You are not *really* that important."

To help dads, in particular, internalize this concept, I will often call a man out of a parent seminar audience and present the following situation:

> Suppose you are a good friend of the boss at your company. It's Friday and you have a need to see him on short notice, so you go over to his office and ask his secretary if you could possibly talk to him for just a few minutes. But the secretary tells you, "I'm sorry, but he's totally booked up until next week on Tuesday—you'll have to come back."
>
> Because you really need to see your boss now, you tell the secretary, "Look, I won't take much of his time. Please just tell him I really need to see him, it'll only take a minute."
>
> And then suppose the secretary tries to call your boss and tell him you're there. She mentions your name, but all she hears back is, "I'm sorry—I simply can't see him now, he'll have to come back next Tuesday."

At this point, I ask my volunteer from the audience the key question: "If this happened to you, how would you feel?"

Invariably, the man replies that he'd feel less important or not very important at all. He would begin to think, *If only I were a vice-president, or somebody who really mattered around here. . . .* The bottom line is that he'd go away thinking, *I'm not important enough.*

And then I simply point out to everyone in the room: "That's exactly how your child feels when you tell him the equivalent of, 'Sorry, come back next Tuesday.'"

It takes effort—and time—to make people feel important. It means inconvenience to make yourself available when you're right in the middle of something. Granted, there are those times when you simply can't stop what you're doing. You can't drop everything to take off with your child or go play a game of catch. But, the point is this: *There are many times when you can stop if you really want to bother.* Stopping on those occasions will help your child realize that you do think he or she is important and, when one of those times comes when you simply can't stop, it won't have the same negative impact that it might have if the child consistently gets the message, "I'm too busy—I can't talk to you or play with you now."

If I Have Not Time, I Am Sounding Brass

A major reason why it's crucial to have time for your children is that if they feel important to you, then they will feel important to their Heavenly Father. Another lesson I learned along the way— probably from Dick Day—is that each one of us earthly fathers models God the Father to our children. You see, God loves your children through you, but if you're not available, how can He love them?

As the chapter title says, **Love Is Spelled T–I–M–E.** You spell acceptance and appreciation the same way. If I say I accept you and love you without conditions, if I say I appreciate you and want you to feel significant, but I spend no time with you, I am exactly like the "sounding brass" the apostle Paul talks about in I Corinthians 13:1. In other words, I don't ring true.

Unfortunately, many parents are falling into the trap of not ringing true to their children and in many cases it's happening by default. Parents wind up being unavailable to their kids because they are too busy. Everyone makes jokes about the hectic pace at which we all seem to be living, but it isn't funny. Parents complain of "having too much to do," and then they tell me about their work schedules, their church schedules, their social schedules. For many people their commuting schedule alone is incredible. They spend several hours a day on the freeway just getting to and from their jobs.

As parents dash through life, too busy to spend time with their children, their children watch and take mental notes. After all, they want to be just like Mom and Dad. And as the years go by, Harry Chapin's song, "The Cat's in the Cradle," comes true. They "grow up just like us."

And then our children will marry, have families of their own, and slip into the same mode, failing to spend enough time with their children, who will be our grandchildren. I often talk to grandparents who have realized their mistake and are now spending more time with their grandchildren than they did with their own children. I believe one of the greatest forces for building better family relationships in our country today is grandparents. I talk to junior high students and ask, "Who can you talk to?" Do you know what they say? Many of them don't mention Mom or Dad. They say, "My grandparents—Grandma or Grandpa."

There are different reasons for this in different families, I'm sure, but one basic reason that kids talk to grandparents more than parents is that Grandma and Grandpa have more time. They're more available.

Are Baby Boomers Better Parents?

According to one study I've seen, fifty years ago the average child had three or four hours a day of interaction with parents or extended family members. But that was in the days when many people lived on farms and the entire family worked together. That was in the days when extended family members lived just down the road.

Today, with our "upwardly mobile" society, people have moved in from the farm to the city or, more correctly, the suburbs. In a typical family, both Mom and Dad dash out the door to work each morning and come dragging back home at night to try getting ready for the next day. The result is that children have only about fifteen minutes of interaction with parents each day. And, according to some experts, twelve of those minutes are spent in a setting where the children hear only critique, instruction, or criticism. That leaves three minutes for fun, laughing together, or enjoying quality moments when real communication occurs.[1]

Today's baby boomer generation of parents likes to talk about spending "quality time" with their kids. The concept of quality time is based upon the idea that, although they have an overpacked scheduled, they can "zero in" and not waste a moment as they relate to and communicate with their children.

According to a report published by *USA Today,* the baby boomer generation (those born between 1946 and 1964) believe that they are doing a better job of parenting than their parents did.[2] Still, study after study shows that these parents are spending far *less* time with their kids than their parents spent with them.

One study of three hundred seventh and eighth graders revealed that children would spend an average of 7.5 minutes a *week* in "focused conversation" with their fathers. Focused conversation means eyeball to eyeball where both people are talking to each other and both people are listening and really exchanging ideas. That's barely *one minute a day* spent really communicating with their fathers. And for mothers, it's not much higher.

Several years ago, I did a conference for six hundred junior high and high school students in one of the largest churches in the United States. The number one question I heard that week was, "Josh, what can I do about my dad?"

"What do your mean?" I would ask.

"Well, he never talks to me. He never takes me anywhere. He never does anything with me."

I spoke sixteen times from Monday noon to Friday noon that week and had forty-two half-hour counseling situations. I could have had three hundred if I had the time, but I handled all I could. At every one of these forty-two sessions, I asked the same question: "Can you talk with your father?"

One student said yes. Forty-one said no.

To Have Quality You Must Have Quantity

I'm convinced that one of the biggest myths we have going today is the myth of "quality time." Of course we all want those quality moments with our kids. But you don't get them by appointment or on some kind of tight schedule. You get quality moments by spending larger quantities of time with your children. Out of the quantity comes the quality.

One of the biggest advantages of quantity time with children is that you are able to serve as a role model for them. Whenever I go downtown, whenever I run an errand, I try to take one of my children with me. If I don't, I miss an opportunity to model for them.

It's when they're with me that they can see how I respond to the world: how I act when another driver cuts me off or when somebody irritates me in some other way.

How do I act when I get cheated, delayed, or frustrated? How do I act, for example, when I put a quarter in the newsstand container and I can't get the door open to get my newspaper? Do I hammer on the thing and call it a few choice names? Or am I patient and able to handle being "ripped off"?

My kids will never know unless they're with me, watching me, experiencing these same frustrations with me. Write this down and seal it in your mind:

> **To be a hero to your kids—a good role model—you have to spend quantity time. And out of that quantity will come the quality that will communicate your acceptance and appreciation of them.**

Disneyland Experiences Won't Do the Job

Another myth we fall victim to is the one that says, "It's the big moments that count." I call them the Disneyland Experiences— those major excursions that take all day and usually cost a lot of money. I used to believe that it was the big moments that counted and I would haul my family to Disneyland or wherever with "great enthusiasm." Finally, Dottie got through to me in her quiet, but laser-accurate way: "Honey, it's not the big times they're going to remember. It's those consistent small moments with them that will mold them and that's what they're really going to remember."

As you can tell, I make it a habit to think about Dottie's remarks. I "check them out" in my mind, and I usually decide that she's right. She wasn't saying that we discontinue the big moments. Disneyland is still on our schedule, but it's not nearly as big as it used to be. Big moments are necessary, but they can never replace the consistent little moments, because it is there that heroes are made and children feel loved and accepted.

What Jim Dobson Taught Me about Teen-Agers

For those who are parents of teen-agers, I'd like to mention still another myth: "The formative years are past." It's amazing how the

Roman Catholic motto, "Give us a child until he is seven" dominates the thinking of society. There is good reason for this, because it's true that the first seven years of life (actually the first three) are very formative ones in many crucial ways. That's why Dick and I emphasize the need for acceptance and building trust and autonomy into a child when he or she is very young.

But recent research is telling us that there is another set of formative years for every child—adolescence, which begins around the age of eleven or twelve. As a child moves into the teen-age years, the myth has it that he doesn't need his parents as much, because he is branching out and becoming independent. Again, there is truth to this, but it's not the whole truth, by any means.

I can recall talking with Dr. James Dobson not long after he published his excellent book, *Preparing for Adolescence*. I mentioned that I had run across so many fathers who thought it was good to spend time with their kids when they were small, but once they got into adolescence, it wasn't that necessary. Dobson's reply was to the effect, "No, that's not right. According to my research, when children reach puberty, they need their parents—especially their fathers—just as much if not more than they ever did."

That little conversation with Jim Dobson gave me new motivation to spend as much time as I could with my own teen-agers and to keep encouraging other fathers to do the same. Yes, I realize this isn't always easy. In fact, in many cases it can seem impossible. When I mention that teen-agers need time with their parents, many moms and dads give me a frustrated look and shrug their shoulders.

"How can we spend time with our teen-agers?" they want to know. "They have their own schedules, their own friends, their own lives. They're almost too busy to talk to us."

I understand, and that's one reason why I urge parents of younger children not to be too busy for their kids. You see, if you start making time for your children when they are very young, you will have many more opportunities—and requests—to spend time with your children when they are teen-agers. At the beginning of this chapter I mentioned Kelly, my sixteen-year-old, who interrupted me while I was writing and wanted me to take her to get her nails done. Many parents would look on such a request as an impertinence or at least a thoughtless imposition. Don't teen-agers know that we parents have better things to do than haul them around?

The answer to that question is "yes and no." Obviously, parents can't sit around and be available on demand every moment of a twenty-four-hour day. There is work to be done, there are chores to take care of. There is a certain schedule to maintain or a family would simply disintegrate into chaos. But at the same time, there are plenty of moments when we can make ourselves available and can allow ourselves to be "imposed upon" if we really are interested in spending more time with our kids. The question every parent must ask is this: **"Is being a parent a major priority for me?"**

I'm not talking about taking an approach to parenting that makes it as a life sentence—a daily duty that every mother and father has to perform. I'm talking about being a hero to your kids— someone who wants to accept, appreciate and nurture them at every opportunity. Spending time with your children is absolutely imperative if you want to be a believable, credible hero who builds your child's security and sense of significance.

As I said in chapter 2, availability just might be the most important "A" of them all in the Positive Parenting Plan. *How can you really accept or appreciate your child if you are not available? How can you show your child affection if you are not there?*

What follows may sound extreme, but we fear that it is all too true:

**If you are not willing to make time
for your children, then everything else
we write in this book is meaningless.**

He Gained Prestige and Lost His Kids

Some of the saddest words that parents ever say is, "If only I had spent more time . . . if only I had listened to my kids more . . . if only. . . ."

The wife of a senior vice-president of a huge construction firm heard me speak at a local church about being available to your children. Later, I ran into this woman in a restaurant. She mentioned hearing my talk, and then she started to cry.

"I have to share something with you," she said hesitantly. "My husband just died. He was a million-dollar-a-year man. He traveled all over the world building and constructing things, but he never took time for his children, even when he was home. All his children turned against him, and when they were grown, they would have nothing to do with him. On his deathbed he confessed to me that he was dying one of the saddest men in the world. He told me, 'I gained prestige, but I lost my family. If only I had spent more time with my children.'"

This widow's words remind me of what Jesus said: "What good will it be for a man if he gains the whole world, yet forfeits his soul? Or what can a man give in exchange for his soul?" (Matthew 16:26, NIV).

Having time for your children will not gain you salvation, but it does indicate how seriously you take the clear advice from Scripture about being a faithful, loving and nurturing parent. This executive died an unhappy man because he had gained the whole world and forfeited his children's love. He made a great deal of money, but he had been unavailable to the most important people in his life. He had bought them things. He had given them birthday cards saying, "I Love You," but they weren't fooled. He should have known: "You can con a con, you can fool a fool, but you can't kid a kid."

As I left that restaurant, memories of that day when I turned my little two-year-old away because I was too busy flooded back. And as I thought of that dad who died without his family's love, Dottie's words took on extra meaning:

If we show an interest in our children now, they will show an interest in us later.

To Think About, Discuss, or Try for Yourself

1.   As a parent, does your day include time for "unscheduled interruptions" by your children? Do you have days when you don't finish your "to-do" list because you've stopped to do other things with your children? Do you consider the time with your kids "wasted" or time well spent?

2.   When you do take time to play with your child, are you patient, or do you sometimes try to hurry the child along?

3.   When Josh tells the story of Kelly's request to take her to have her nails done just as he is in the middle of an important project, he describes three thoughts that flash through his mind. Which thought is the most useful and why?

4.   According to this chapter, when you are not available to your children, what does it say to them?

5.   How do parents fall into the trap of "not ringing true" to their children? Is this happening to you? Talk with your spouse about the schedule both of you are keeping. Do you schedule adequate time for the children? If not, how can adequate time be scheduled in?

6.   According to this chapter, what is the only way to have adequate "quality time" with your kids? How much quality time would you estimate that you have with the children each day? Each week?

7.   Toward the end of this chapter, Josh claims that if parents are not willing to make time for their children, then everything else in this book is meaningless. Do you agree or disagree? Why?

8.   Ask your spouse to join with you in both writing your own paragraphs concerning how you feel about Dottie McDowell's statement, "If we show an interest in our children now, they will show an interest in us later." After writing your paragraphs, exchange your papers and then discuss what you have said.

12

How to "Hone In" on Your Kids

THE FEATURE writer for a major Christian magazine was well into interviewing our family for a cover story when she asked our son, Sean: "What is the one thing you don't like about your dad?"

Sean, who was around six or seven at the time, gave the lady a puzzled look and said, "Nothing."

"There has to be *something*," the woman coaxed. "Tell me *one* thing."

"Well . . ." said Sean slowly, "He's away from home a lot. . . ."

The reporter's eyes widened a bit and she hastily scribbled some notes, but made no comment. Then she went on to talk to the rest of us and was about to leave when I stopped her.

"Would you mind calling Sean back in and asking him one more question?"

"Why no," said the writer. "But what do you want me to ask?"

"Ask him, 'What do you like most about your dad?'"

"I don't see why . . ." she began.

"Just ask him," I said with a smile. "Let's see what happens."

She called Sean back into the room and asked him the question, "Sean, what do you like most about your dad?"

Without hesitation Sean replied, "He spends a lot of time with me."

The feature writer included Sean's remark in her notes, but I could tell she wasn't quite putting it together. I hadn't insisted that she ask the other children that question, and she was wondering why we had gone through this little exercise with Sean.

"In case you're wondering why I wanted you to do that," I said to her, "remember when you asked him 'What is one thing you don't like about your dad'? He was kind of backed in a corner on that one, but I really liked his answer. He told you the one thing he *didn't* like about me was that I'm away from home a lot. The first time that my being away from home *isn't* something he dislikes about me, then I'm in trouble."

The feature writer gave me a puzzled look, so I continued: "You see, if Sean didn't mind my being away, that would mean that when I'm home we don't have much going for us, but he *wants* me to be home, because we spend a lot of time together and enjoy one another."

The lady thanked me and left. Later, when her story came out, she had covered the part about Sean's likes and dislikes about his father very well. And I think it made the best point in the article.

"Early to Bed" Is More Than a Motto

I'm sure our other children could have said the same as Sean concerning what they don't like about their dad. I *am* on the road a lot, but over the years I have compensated for my unavoidable schedule in at least two ways:

1. I have my family travel with me as often as possible, especially during the summers. As a result, we're together a good deal of the time despite my having to be on the road so much.

2. When my two oldest children, Kelly and Sean, were younger, I had a policy that some people thought was rather odd. No matter who was visiting or telephoning or whatever it might be, I would excuse myself and go to bed with the children.

If we were having guests over, they were told ahead of time, "At 6:30 or 7:00 Josh will be unavailable." We also told people, "Don't phone Josh between 6:30 and 9:00 P.M. because he'll be with the children."

When I was home, I would try to take those two and a half hours every evening and spend them with Kelly and Sean. You may be wondering where Dottie was. Some of the time, she was taking a well-deserved break. With her husband on the road that much, she deserved one! (For that matter, she still does.)

What did the children and I do every night? It sometimes was as simple as going for a walk, reading a book, or wrestling on the floor.

One of our favorite activities was getting in the jacuzzi that had been installed in our bedroom. The jacuzzi was a very special gift from friends.

On many evenings, the kids and I got in the jacuzzi first and Dottie would often join us later. One night just for fun we filled a giant Tupperware bowl with popcorn and floated it in the water. It swirled around and around and everybody had ample opportunity to dip in. The kids talked about that one for weeks and I even heard back from teachers and other dads about the "popcorn in the jacuzzi."

Sometimes we watched TV while we were in the jacuzzi, and one of our favorite shows was "Family Feud." The kids loved to see if our family could outdo the two families who competed on the program.

Granted, my "heading for bed" every night by 6:30 or 7:00 sounds extreme, and I suppose it was. I'm afraid I offended a few people, or at least caused them to question my sanity. But I also received letters that said things like, "What I have learned most from your life when visiting your home was that you went off to bed early to spend time with your children." Or someone would write—often a college student—and say: "After all the times I've heard you speak, I've gotten more from hearing you say, 'Please excuse me, I'm going to bed with my kids.'"

"Early to Rise" Is for Heroes, Too

Over the years my schedule had varied a great deal. Recently, while finishing up one major book project, I got up around 2:00 A.M. and worked at my desk until 6:00. Then I would wake up the children and they would all jump in bed with me where we would wrestle, talk, and discuss what they were going to be doing that day. Then we would all get dressed, have breakfast, and I would drive them to school.

A ritual I tried to maintain over the years, if at all possible, was to take all the children out after school the first day I was home from a trip. I would pick them up around 2:30, and we'd all go out for a one-hour date. Then, for the next four days, I would take the children individually on one-hour dates—have a yogurt, an ice cream soda, or whatever they wanted. The point is, we'd go out and play for a solid hour, doing whatever each child wanted to do. Often they would bring a friend along.

What I've just described about evenings, mornings and afternoons with my children may sound like overkill to some parents. They might say, "How does he have time for all that?"

Keep in mind that I don't constantly hold to any particular regimen. I've described above some different routines that I have followed for certain periods of time over the years. A lot depends on my current schedule, as well as the ages of my children at the time. Today, for example, with Kelly and Sean in high school, and Katie in elementary school and Heather in kindergarten, I have to do different things to meet everyone's needs.

The point is, every family is different and everyone's schedule is different. Because my schedule keeps me on the road much of the time, I work very hard at honing in on my kids when I'm at home. This, however, causes me other problems because in trying to spend time with the children I sometimes leave Dottie feeling she hasn't had enough time with me. So I constantly keep working at honing in on her as well. It's a constant struggle, but I have learned that it all can work. I *can* be a hero to my wife and kids. I *can* be available to my family—*if I want to be.* I have also learned that parenting can be one of the most fulfilling and emotionally satisfying experiences in life.

Do What Fits Your Style, Not Mine

To be an available hero you don't have to spend a lot of money or do things that are complicated or not your style, but you do have to spend enough time. I am mentioning several of the things I do with my children in this chapter, some of which may seem pretty far out, but the point is, *I'm spending time with my children my way.* You can do the same—*your way.*

The key is to be sure you spend *time.* It doesn't have to be doing something out of the ordinary—in fact, doing ordinary things with your kids is usually all they want. Your long-range goal should be developing a mind set that never wavers.

**Make it your commitment to do things
with your kids and never fail to keep that commitment.**

I often ask at parent seminars, "How many of you have gotten sleeping bags and gone out in the backyard to 'camp out' for the night with your kids?" I've done it, and I know what kind of conversations you can have out there alone gazing up at the stars. It's then that kids will talk about things and share with you. This is one of our favorite activities when we are at the beach for a few days.

Whenever possible, I like to hone in on each child, one on one. One summer, while we were at a ranch in the back country of Idaho, on a trip given to us as a gift, I asked Sean, "Son, how would you like to go off alone somewhere just with me?"

Sean was all for it, and we got some knapsacks, packed some lunches, took along some Cokes, and headed out for what turned out to be a five-hour excursion.

We walked back up a canyon and found this waterfall where we could go swimming in a pool, sun on the rocks, eat our lunch, and just be together. We even convinced ourselves we were the first human beings who had ever come that way. (On the way back, however, we found several cans and bottles that told us that wasn't quite true.)

But all in all it was a great time—five hours to hone in and concentrate on my son, who was ten years of age that year. I still look back on it as the highlight of that summer, something Disneyland, or Knott's Berry Farm, or any of the high-powered expensive amusement parks couldn't begin to match.

An Early Saturday Water-Balloon Battle

Always, my goal is to do things with my kids that I was never able to do with my father because he never wanted to. Maybe I'm fulfilling some of my childhood dreams, but I believe it's a healthy way to go about it. For example, I always wanted to have a water-balloon fight with my dad and mom, but they never would do it. A few years back, on Easter weekend I said, "Kids, how would you like to have a water-balloon fight?" They couldn't believe I was willing to do it, but when I brought out a hundred and twenty balloons and began filling them with water, they knew I meant business.

After I filled all the balloons, our two children (we had Kelly and Sean at the time) and two of their friends came out in the yard with me. I took a garden hose and formed a giant circle out of it. Then I gave each child thirty balloons filled with water and stood in the center of the big circle. There was one rule; only one child could throw a balloon at a time, but the moment that balloon broke somebody else could throw another one. The other rule was that every time someone hit me that child got a quarter. But every time I caught the balloon and fired it back and hit them they had to give me a nickel.

What followed can only be described as forty-five minutes of sheer pandemonium and fun. And I still believe what we did was very biblical. Ecclesiastes tells us there are times to laugh and to dance (3:4). The prophet Zachariah wrote of parents whose hearts were glad and their children seeing it and being joyful (10:7).

The point is, something like a water balloon fight on Easter break makes memories that children don't forget. And making those indelible memories is what being a hero is all about.

Try Going for a Walk—Backwards!

What I'm going to suggest next may not be for you, but it's another idea that you can adapt to fit your own style. Have you ever walked around the block *backwards* while talking to your child? If you're a little weird and crazy the way I am, you may want to try it because it's certainly a different experience.

Granted, when the neighbors see you walking backwards, they might think that you have finally flipped, but your kids will love it. You're walking backwards while they're looking at you as they walk forward. For the first block or so, there is a lot of giggling and laughing, but then I try to slip in some spiritual truths. For example: "Jesus is the light of the world and wherever we walk, He shows us where to go, He shows us what life is all about."

If walking backwards isn't your thing, obviously you can walk forward with your child just to talk and share. You can walk down to the corner to get an ice cream cone. If the supermarket isn't too far away, you can walk down there to pick up some groceries. The important thing is:

Take your children along whenever you go anywhere in order to spend time communicating and sharing.

As I mentioned in chapter 11, I seldom run an errand by myself. I always take one of my children along so we can talk and I can ask them how they're doing and what they think about certain things, certain people, certain events that have happened in the news. Sometimes I have to run down to the city of Ramona, which is around thirty-five minutes away, at the base of the mountain. I always take a child with me and I can't remember a time I didn't spend part of the trip at least talking with them about something of interest.

If I Don't Plan It, It Won't Happen

You may think all of this is easy for Josh McDowell—that he's some sort of super dad who just loves jumping in jacuzzis, walking backwards and dashing off with his kids every five minutes to talk and chat and have fun together. Actually, *I have to work at it all the time,* even to the point of planning what I'm going to talk about with my children.

You see, when I spend time with my kids, I don't want to count on "just letting communication happen." I suppose some dads might not have a problem, but someone like me—an extravert whose mind runs a mile a minute—has to be careful. If I don't plan what I'm going to talk about, even down to the questions I'm going to ask my children, not a whole lot may happen.

For example, if I take one of the kids along for a ride down the mountain to Ramona, it would be easy to spend the entire round trip sitting there thinking about all the projects I'm working on—books, video scripts, television programs, messages that I'm going to give on my next speaking tour. I could think of all that and wind up not talking to my son or daughter at all.

Another thing I have learned is that if I don't plan time with my children, intrusions and interruptions can take over and I never get much time with them. When I plan ahead of time what we're going to be doing and when, it helps me to hone in and get my mind focused on them and what we'll be doing. I know some people might have no problem focusing, but I believe that for a lot of men, in particular, it's hard, especially for the busy businessman who has an awful lot on his mind. I suppose working at communicating and planning what you'll talk about sound a little cut and dried. Sometimes it seems that way to me, but I do it anyway because it gets me going and helps me be faithful in being available to my children.

Develop the Art of Asking Questions

Something I work at very hard is asking my children questions that can get a conversation going. I'll do this driving in the car, walking, or just sitting at the table at meal time. Some of the questions I've asked include:

"If you could change our family, how would you change it?" (You better be ready on that one.)

"If you were the father of the family, what would you do differently?" (You better be ready on that one, too!)

"What have you always wanted to do that we have never done together as a family?"

You might want to read Proverbs 15:13 and 17:22, where it talks about happiness and sadness and then ask: "When was the time you were happiest? The time you were saddest? What makes you happy? What makes you sad?" These questions can lead to a good discussion together.

Once after we'd been to the zoo, we had a fairly long ride home and I didn't want to waste the time. As we left the parking lot, I said, "Kids, let's play a little game. What animal did you see today that best describes you and why?"

For the next sixty miles, Dottie and I got tremendous insights as to what our kids think about themselves. Little Katie—she was about three and a half at the time—said she believed she was like the bears.

"Why?" I wanted to know.

"Because I like to be hugged," Katie chirped.

Katie was in the back seat, so I pulled over, got out of the car and went around to open her door so I could give her a great big bear hug before we continued with our trip.*

Being a Hero to Their Friends

When I go on "dates" with my kids, I don't always hone in on them alone. When I'm home long enough, after a few days, I allow them to bring at least one friend along because I want my children to see how I act around their friends. I want their friends to see I'm fun to be around, and sometimes *that* can take some interesting twists! In fact, it can bring me out of my shell in a hurry. On one occasion my daughter Kelly had a friend over and they started pestering me about "doing my hair."

"Oh, no, you don't really want to do my hair," I protested.

"Come on, Dad," Kelly pleaded.

I saw Kelly's friend eyeing me, wondering what I'd do. Would I really take the risk? Finally, maybe my pride won out. I had always

---

* For more ideas on what to ask or talk about, see Appendix, p. 219.

said I wanted to be a hero to my daughter's friends, so why not go for broke?

"Okay," I told them. "You can do my hair any way you want to, but you can't cut it or dye it and you both have to agree to go out to dinner with me afterward."

"All *right!*" they both shrieked, and for the next hour or so they went at it with mousse, hair dryer and a few other tools I didn't recognize. When they finished, they had my hair sticking out in every direction. I looked like a flying saucer, ready to take off for a distant planet. As I gazed into the mirror, I thought twice about the other end of the deal. Did I really want to go out to dinner in public? I could only hope that no one would recognize me!

When we walked into the local pizza parlor, dark glasses and all, the girls stayed about five feet behind, because they didn't want anybody to know they were with me! People did stare, but no one called the police and we had a great time.

When we got back and Sean heard about it, he felt left out. "Can my buddy and I do your hair, too?" he wanted to know. I looked at Sean and wondered what kind of precedent I had set.

"Tomorrow night, but the deal is you've got to go out to dinner with me."

Next evening Sean and his buddy took a whole hour working on my hair and, basically, they succeeded in making a mess out of it. They were happy with their creation, however, and, as agreed, we went out to dinner—but this time, I chose another restaurant, thinking the pizza parlor couldn't handle me two nights in a row.

My crazy hairdos made me something of a legend in my own time around Julian. For weeks afterward teachers stopped me downtown as well as other people to tell me they had "heard about my hair." I just laughed because I had accomplished my objective. My kids had fun with me and so did their friends. We had talked, laughed, and just had a good time together. I had always said I wanted to be a dad who was willing to try anything, and this time I had put my hair where my mouth was.

What Are They into Right Now?

If you really want to step into your child's world, you've got to keep abreast of what your child is into right now. That is, what's "hot" with your kids at the moment? As I've been working on this book, the big thing for my ten-year-old daughter, Katie, is "doing lunch" with her dad on school days. The last time I was home, I took Katie out for lunch twice in five days. Often, I'll bring her one single rose as my special token of affection. Once she came to me and asked, "Can we go on a buggy ride? I want to go on a buggy ride just with you."

I told Katie I'd see what I could do. The next day I hired a buggy and driver and we pulled up just as school was letting out. When Katie came out and saw the buggy, her eyes got as big as saucers. All of her friends crowded around as she got in and we rode off together to have lunch. I have a hunch Katie won't forget that particular buggy ride.

For Sean right now, the big thing in life is basketball. Last summer, Dottie and I sent Sean off to a basketball camp, and while he was gone I had a contractor help me pour a concrete pad and put up a goal. When Sean got back from camp, he didn't know what to be thrilled about the most—going to camp or having the new court where he could practice all the moves he had learned.

We had a great time, and I wanted to know all about what had happened. What kind of players had been there? Who had been the best player there? It turned out Sean had been named one of the best players in camp, despite the fact he was one of the shortest.

"Dad, you wouldn't believe how *big* some of those guys were," Sean exclaimed.

We have some great talks about basketball. And in this case it's easy to enter my child's world because basketball was one of my favorite sports in high school, where I started on the varsity team as a sophomore. Sean came to me not long ago and said, "Dad, I don't think I'll be able to start for Julian High as a sophomore. . . ."

"Sean," I told him. "I want you to know it makes no difference to me if you start for your team, if you sit on the bench and never get to play, or if you don't play basketball at all. All I want is that you'll participate in what you want to do and that you'll enjoy it. It's great that you got named one of the best players in camp. It's great if you can make the team. But what's really great is that you're my son and I appreciate you for that first and foremost."

Recording Their Lives on Calendars

I've shared a lot of things I do with our children as I try to be available to them.* I could share just as many things that Dottie does,

---

* For additional ideas, see Appendix, p. 219.

but one of her projects is so special it deserves substantial description. Dottie enters into the world of her own children by keeping a record of each child's life on monthly calendars. I'm talking about those calendars that have at least a one inch square for each day of the month and into those squares Dottie puts brief but special notations about what happened that day and what it meant to the child and the rest of the family.

Every year Dottie buys four calendars, one for each of our children. She tries to pick out photographic themes that fit each child. For example, one year Sean was into biking so she bought a calender with pictures of ten-speed bike events. Because Sean's current big interest is basketball, this year he has a basketball calendar.

Kelly, Sean's older sister, seems to be into everything so Dottie wound up buying her a calendar that has a lot of pictures depicting shopping—a favorite sport of most teen-agers. Katie, our ten-year-old, loves horses, so you know what is featured on her calendar.

Little Heather, only four years old, loves cats and, naturally, every month of her calendar has another picture of cats or kittens.

As each month unfolds, Dottie tries to fill in each day with a brief synopsis of what the child has done, what happened of note, and other brief remembrances. She doesn't always manage to cover each day, but she fills in an amazing number of days every month for all of our kids.

The notations are simple ones—sometimes that even sound a bit mundane—but they're very meaningful to the children and to us their parents. For example here are some entries from last fall:

Heather—you went to school today. Daddy picked you up after school and you went to the drugstore for an ice cream sundae.
Katie—our family is having a huge garage sale behind the drugstore. Tonight I took you down to your soccer game in Ramona. It was so close and exciting—your team lost 2-1.

Then the next day's entry read:

You helped Dad and me at our family garage sale. Then you and I watched Boston lose the second playoff game with the Oakland A's.
Sean—you got voted president of your freshman class today. I am soooooooo proud of you! Luke came home with you to spend the night. He killed a scorpion that we found.
Kelly—you did clothes shopping for school today and found some great stuff.

Along with making the notations on the squares for the day of the month, Dottie collects snapshots, certificates, news clippings, ribbons, and any other items that help record what the children accomplished or happened to them during the month. All of this memorabilia gets clipped, taped, or pasted on the photo/picture page that appears above the days of the given month.

As each month passes, the scenes of cats, horses, basketball players, or shopping slowly disappear as Dottie adds a record of what has happened in the lives of our kids. You could say her calendar serves the same purpose as a scrap book, but there is something intriguing about recording things day by day. It helps remind all of us of the value and meaning of time and how even the simplest things make up what life is really all about.

Like the notations, the photos and other memorabilia are often simple—but priceless. For example:

Heather is pictured with her friends at a birthday party and there is also a special picture of a new friend she made that month.

Katie is pictured with her softball team and there is also a photo of her appearing in a style show, where she won a ribbon. The ribbon is there too, to remind her of her accomplishment.

Sean is pictured with two different basketball teams he was playing on at the time. And along with those photos are some illustrations he drew for the science fair where he won a first-place ribbon.

On Kelly's calendar is a picture of Kelly with her "new car"— a 1957 Chevy that she got for a steal. If you're into cars at all you know that '57 Chevys are something of a "classic," but what's more important is that this photo records a classic time in Kelly's life— when she got her license and her own wheels and started using new freedoms and responsibilities.

Tucked in the back of every calendar are photos and other items that Dottie hasn't had time to record yet. But she works on her project every day—for at least ten minutes, when she makes her notations and tries to sort out photos and other items to display in their proper places. Dottie says that the calendars aren't a chore, but something that she really enjoys. I asked her what she might say for this book regarding the calendars and their value and she told me:

> I would say the calendars are one of my biggest priorities because they're something that give us and the kids an invaluable record. I've often thought about when I would give these calendars to the

children. When they get married? No, I don't think so. I believe I'll give them the calendars when they have children of their own. When they get married, they'll be so busy getting their homes together the calendars might be lost in the shuffle, but when they have children, then they'll realize the incredible value of a record like this.

The reason I got started was because I was given a baby shower gift when Heather came—a calendar with the stickers that said, "The first time I sat up," "The first time I smiled," and so on. I got such a kick out of filling out those stickers for Heather I decided to start making calendar records for all the other children, and that's what I've been doing ever since.

I admit the calendars are a lot of work, but they are also a lot of fun. As I collect the different years, I can see month by month how the children grow, what they were into, what their interests were, what they left behind and what they continued on to do. There's tremendous satisfaction in that.

Keeping a calendar record for each of your children may be a bit too ambitious for your particular schedule right now. Then again, it may be something you might want to try. You could start on a modest basis and see what happens. What we have discovered is that the children are as interested in the calendars as we are. Sean in particular likes to bring his friends home, get out the calendars, and show them what his mother has recorded. You can see the pride sparkle in his eyes as he shares this precious record of his life with his friends.

Sean doesn't really understand how precious it is, but he does understand one thing: The calendars represent his mother's consuming interest in his life as well as the lives of his sisters. They remind him of what he and his family do together, they remind him of our availability and willingness to be involved in his life. And what could be more important than that?

To Think About, Discuss, or Try for Yourself

The last thing you should do with this chapter is just think or talk about the ideas. Instead, pick several ideas that appeal to you and *try doing them* with your children. If something doesn't click, don't get discouraged. Modify the idea or change it completely. The important thing is to make doing things together with your kids *a way of life.*

Part VI

Accountability
and Authority:
How Limits Develop
Self-Discipline and
Self-Decisiveness

In Parts II through V, we have described what goes into a loving relationship: *acceptance, appreciation, affection,* and *availability.* As you establish that loving relationship, *Limits* must come into play. While it is true that *Limits* without *Love* can cause rebellion, it is equally true that all *Love* and no *Limits* can cause just as many problems, and, in some cases, even more.

The *Limits* half of parenting includes two more A's in the Positive Plan for Parenting. The first is *accountability,* which simply means "willing and able to be called to account, to explain or answer for your actions in a responsible way." Accountability helps the child develop self-discipline.

Finally, we have *authority,* the parameters with which children learn the moral attributes of God, and concepts of right and wrong. Authority helps the child learn to make choices within certain boundaries. Authority helps the child become self-decisive.

As we will see, accountability and authority overlap as one builds upon and blends with the other. Key concepts and ideas will include:

- why accountability is vital to a happy family
- how accountability, submission, and obedience go together
- why secure people are better equipped to submit and be accountable
- the best way to teach your kids to be responsible
- what can happen when you are willing to be accountable to your spouse and children
- how to go beyond "good intentions"

- why being accountable makes discipline easier in those "sticky situations"
- why you are not responsible for your kids
- why accountable parents aren't afraid to be challenged
- how autocratic parenting crushes the spirit
- why permissiveness leads to chaos
- how "having it all" can lead to indifference toward your children
- why relational, authoritative parenting is best for everyone
- how boundaries help children learn to make better choices
- principles for operating as a relational parent
- the secret to making logical consequences work every time
- the four hardest words any parent can say
- how to do a "magnet check" on everyone's emotions
- why being a hero never stops.

13

Accountable Parents Raise Accountable Kids

As I travel the country speaking to parents' groups, I often hear complaints about kids who are "irresponsible." One father with three children in grade school told me:

"Josh, I really like what you say about being accepting, loving, and available, and all the rest, but somewhere along the way, the rubber has to meet the road. Kids have to learn to mind—and be responsible. What I'd like to know is how to teach my kids *responsibility*. If I didn't get on their cases, they'd never clean their rooms, take out the garbage, or do any of the simple little chores I assign them."

I sympathized with that father because he was telling it like it is. As we talked, it was apparent that he had done much to develop a relationship with his children. On a scale of 1 to 10, his "hero image" was at least a 7.5—maybe higher. But his kids, being human, weren't that crazy about being responsible—or what I also call accountable.

Concepts like accountability and responsibility aren't really that popular, especially with children. After all, being accountable can cramp your style. It's easier to do your own thing and not have to answer to anyone. But that's not how life works. Without accountability, society would be in shambles. Without accountability, homes can degenerate into chaos—and many do because a family member refuses to act responsibly toward the rest of the family.

Accountability Involves Submission and Obedience

I believe accountability is closely associated with two biblical concepts—submission and obedience. If I am willing to be accountable, that means I am humble enough to submit to others and obey, please, or serve them.

A lot of people think submission has something to do with being a doormat or a wimp. When the apostle Paul listed ways to live out being filled with the Spirit, he said, "Submit to one another out of reverence to Christ" (Ephesians 5:31, NIV). I especially like the way Dick Day puts it:

Submission: Not asserting your own needs over someone else's, but rather endeavoring to meet the other person's needs by ministering to the other person through the principles taught in 1 Corinthians 13

Becoming accountable and responsible is a crucial part of growing up and becoming a mature, balanced human being. To be accountable means submitting to others and ministering to their needs rather than always being worried about yours. Learning to be accountable—and responsible—is one important way anyone learns to put away childish things and become a mature man or woman.

To submit or be accountable takes a secure person who knows he is accepted, a person who feels significant because he has been shown genuine appreciation. If we accept and appreciate our kids, they can learn to be accountable. In fact, I believe they will *want* to be accountable!

Me? Be Accountable to My Kids?

Whenever a dad or a mom asks me how they can teach the kids responsibility, my answer is always the same: "Have you ever tried becoming accountable to your kids?"

Most parents are puzzled at first, and wonder what I mean by asking *them* to be accountable to their kids. After all, the kids are the ones who need to learn to be more accountable to the parents. Isn't that what responsibility is all about?

I agree that children need to learn responsibility, but I have become convinced that the best way to train children to be accountable and responsible is to set the example yourself, *by being accountable to them.*

I'm not suggesting that you put the children in charge—far from it. What I am suggesting is that you be humble and submissive enough to give your children permission to "call you to account" when you act in an unloving, irresponsible manner.

True, they may not always be fair in what they think is "unloving," and they may often see things from their child's point of view, but making yourself accountable to your children provides an invaluable bridge of communication between the two of you. As the child watches you be accountable, he will learn to be accountable. I have found no better way to teach accountability than through role-modeling it before my children.

How I Got Help from an Expert

When my children were small, I realized I needed help with being accountable, so I went to the most knowledgeable person I know—my wife. There is no one on earth who even comes close to loving me as much as Dottie. No one respects and admires me more than the one who shares her life and her love with me—the mother of my children, my sweetheart, my best friend, and the special gift God gave me.

And so I said to her, "Honey, I need your help. Will you hold me accountable as a husband and a father? If I'm on the road too much, tell me. If I'm not meeting your needs or the children's needs, spell it out for me. If I'm not spending time with the children or spending time with you—I want to know about it."

"Okay, Josh," Dottie replied, just a little bit reluctantly. "I'll tell you, but sometimes it may hurt a little."

"Honey, I know I'm probably going to get defensive sometimes, but when I do, you have the right to tell me that, too. I want to hear the truth."

But I wasn't through. When Kelly's seventh birthday rolled around, I put a special note in her birthday card from me:

Dear Kelly, I sure love you. I count it such a joy to be your dad, but you know, I'm going to need your help this year. I've never been the father of a seven-year-old daughter before. I just want to be the best dad I can be to you. And if you ever feel that I'm not doing right or not being fair, or loving and considerate, please tell me.

When Sean turned seven, I did the same thing with him. In fact, I've done it with all the children. With Katie I said, "I've never been the father of a seven-year-old, blue-eyed blonde before." And Heather is learning from her older siblings the value of accountability among all of us as a family.

Kids Aren't Afraid to Hold You Accountable

Ever since I've asked them for help on being accountable, my wife and kids have become my best counselors. Kelly and Sean, for example, accepted my proposition with enthusiasm. In chapter 2, I mentioned the "gag bag" incident and how Kelly corrected me. But the other kids have put in their two cents' worth on many occasions. For example, Sean and I were walking along the street downtown one day when a man stopped us to talk to me. Something he said irritated me and I was rather short with him. As the man walked away, Sean remarked, "Dad, you were very short with that man. You didn't talk to him very nicely."

I felt like dying right there on the street. We ran after the man, who was still in sight, and when we caught up I stopped him. With my son standing right there with me, I apologized for my rude behavior.

Just a few months ago, I got back from a trip and was approached by our ten-year-old daughter Katie, who said firmly: "Daddy, you're not being fair to me."

"What do you mean, honey?"

"When you come home from trips, you take Kelly and Sean and Heather out, but not me."

"Really?"

"Yes," my ten-year-old said unflinchingly, and then she added, "Will you take me out for lunch today?"

I was glad Katie had the freedom to hold me accountable by telling me she thought I was being unfair. I thought I had been spending enough time with her, but apparently she hadn't seen it that way, and I was more than happy to oblige her request for lunch. In fact, as I noted in chapter 12, lunch has become a big thing for Katie at this point in her life, and we've been "doing lunch" a lot during the past year.

Being Accountable Can Get Uncomfortable

Please understand that being accountable to my family hasn't been any easier for me than it would be for any other parent. I'm not saying that Dottie or any of the children take advantage of my offer to be open to their correction, but they also aren't shy about giving me some "tips."

Sometimes their critiques sting and I get defensive. Every time I become defensive, however, it only causes them to clam up, and there goes my greatest source of insight and help. So I have learned that while there are moments when I might have to choke on my pride as I swallow it in big chunks, I do it anyway because I know I can't get along without the invaluable help that Dottie and the children give me when they hold me accountable. If I have learned anything as a father and a husband, it's this:

Good intentions don't automatically become reality.

Long ago I realized that as I look at my life, I judge myself based on my intentions—but that doesn't necessarily get the job done. As someone has observed, the road to a very hot place is paved with good intentions. My wife and children, however, have the right to judge me on my actions—*how I follow through on my intentions*. It seems that at least once every week or so someone reminds me that I have some work to do if I want to make my good intentions become reality.

Besides having your pride hurt and getting defensive now and then, there are other dangers to being accountable. For example, you can get criticized by people outside your family. The Christian man is supposed to be the "authority figure" in his home. He is supposed to be the "strong leader" who guides and protects his family under all kinds of conditions. How then can the husband and father allow his wife and children to challenge him?

I simply tell my critics that I believe I am a servant-leader who is strong enough to be able to say to Dottie and the kids, "I want you to hold me accountable. If I'm not cutting the mustard in your eyes, let me know."

I believe a leader is the one who is strong enough to say, "Help me. *I need your help.* I want to be all that God wants me to be as your husband, as your father."

Accountability and Role-Modeling Go Together

In chapter 12 I mentioned how I try to take at least one child along when I go on any kind of errand, no matter how brief it might be. My major goal is to communicate with my kids, to relate to them—and to model for them when possible.

I recall one occasion when I asked Sean if he wanted to drive down to the shopping center with me to get some tape at the hardware store. At first he said no, but then he said yes because he knew I would buy him an ice cream cone on the way back.

We got in the car and started out. It was only about an eight-minute drive down to the shopping center, but as we were driving along, I reached over and rubbed Sean's shoulders and said, "You know, son, you're really special to me. I just want to let you know I count it such a privilege to be your dad. I'm one of the luckiest men in the world. I know a lot of boys in this world, but of all the boys I know there is no one I'd rather have as my son than you."

Sean looked up at me and said, "*Really,* Dad?"

"Really," was all I said as I pulled into a parking place at the shopping center. I'd been so busy talking with Sean that I didn't notice I'd parked almost right in the center of two parking places instead of between the lines for one. I was halfway out of the car when I noticed, and for a second it was tempting to just leave the car where it was because we were in a bit of a hurry. But then I told myself, *No, this could mean somebody else would have to walk farther because they can't find a parking place—what kind of role-modeling is that for your son?*

I told Sean to stay put for just a second. Then as I started to back up, I realized that here was a good opportunity to do a little teaching, along with setting an example.

"Son, do you know why I'm backing up?"

"Why, Dad?" he wanted to know.

"Well, you can see I didn't do a very good job of parking, in fact, I took up two places. In 1 Corinthians 13 it talks about how love is considerate of other people. It would be rude to leave the car parked like this. Somebody else might not be able to find a place, and they'd have to walk a lot farther to get to the store. And that's why I'm backing up, so I can park the car right before we go in."

Sean didn't say anything, and I just dropped it. But I had accomplished my goal. The opportunity to model and teach had been there and I had grabbed it.

Being Accountable Makes Discipline Easier

Being accountable to your kids can put you in some tight spots, but it also lays groundwork for following through with discipline when it really counts. If you have been accountable before your children, it will be easier to hold them accountable when those sticky situations pop up.

I don't know about you, but at our house, the sticky situations pop up quite often. By a "sticky situation," I mean something that may not look so critical, but if you let it go, it only sets a pattern that teaches the child that, "It's okay to be irresponsible some of the time." I have learned that when you let enough of these things go, it only undermines whatever you've been trying to teach regarding responsibility.

One morning I came into the kitchen and saw that Sean had left for school without taking out the garbage. Garbage detail is his daily assignment, which is clearly described as having to be done before he leaves for school each morning.

"I've got to go get him and bring him back so he can take out the garbage," I told Dottie.

"Josh," Dottie said in dismay. "You can't. It's time for school to start in just a few minutes. He'll be penalized."

"Honey, I've got to do it. He can't learn any other way. I have to hold him accountable to do what he said he would do."

I got in the car and drove down to the school—two miles away. The bell hadn't quite rung and Sean was still on the playground, shooting baskets with some of his buddies. I called him over and said, "Son, I want you to get your bike and head back up to the house and do the garbage."

"But, Dad," Sean protested. "It's five minutes to the bell. Can't I do it after school?"

"No, son, you were supposed to do it before you left for school, and I'd like you to go do it right now, please."

"Dad, couldn't you do it for me—just once?"

"No, son, it's your responsibility. Please ride up and take care of it."

Sean flipped the ball back to his buddies and trudged over to his bike, shoulders slumping. As he rode away, it was a tough moment. A little voice whispered in my ear, *What kind of dad are you, McDowell? It wouldn't hurt to take out the garbage for your son just once, would it?*

I had to admit that the little voice had something there. Of course I could have done it for him in a minute, but it was his responsibility, and for me to do his chore wouldn't really be helpful at all. In fact, in the long run it could harm him because it could teach that, "A little irresponsibility is okay."

By the time Sean got up to the house, took out the garbage and rode back town to school, the bell had rung, and he was a good thirty minutes late for class. The teacher had seen him leave the school yard, a direct violation of a strict rule and, not understanding why, he sent Sean to the principle's office.

"Sean, why did you leave the school yard and wind up a half hour late for class?" the principal asked.

Sean told the principle what had happened—how he'd had to ride back home to do the garbage because his dad had come all the way down to school to let him know that he had forgotten. The principal sat quietly—actually, he was a bit speechless—and after Sean finished, he said, "Thank you, Sean, for telling me this. You may go back to class now. I'll talk with your teacher about this later."

A few minutes later, the principal called me. "I can't believe what Sean just told me. I want you to know how much we appreciate this. At first, I thought Sean was into some kind of monkey business, but when he told me what happened, I was tremendously impressed. We only wish more parents would hold their kids accountable. It would make our job so much easier. I'll tell Sean's teacher what really happened, and in this case, he's excused because he had a parent's permission to leave the school and go home."

As I hung up the phone, I felt a tremendous surge of relief. I had felt like an ogre for being that picky about one bag of garbage, but the principal's words had reassured me.

That happened last fall—when Sean was thirteen. I wish I could say he's never missed a bag of garbage in the morning since, but at least I can report he hasn't missed too many!

The Case of the Generous Shoplifter

On another occasion, Sean and two of his buddies wanted to ride downtown with Dottie and me because they wanted to pick up a few items at a variety store. Katie, who was around five at the time, wanted to come too. She went along with the boys into the store while Dottie and I remained in the car, going over some "to do" lists together.

When the children finally came back out, Katie was carrying several little items—some lapel pins and some very colorful pencils. She handed the pins and the pencils to Sean's two friends, saying, "I bought these things for you."

Without thinking too much about it at the moment, Dottie and I nodded approvingly, and commented that it was nice to be thoughtful of others. But as we drove on down the street, Dottie began thinking, *Where did Katie get the money to buy those things?*

Dottie asked me to stop the car, and the two of us asked Katie to get out and go for a short walk with us. While the boys waited in the car, we quizzed her and discovered that she had shoplifted the gifts she had given the boys.

"Honey, it's not right to take things that you don't pay for," Dottie explained. "You have to get them back from the boys and we'll have to take them back to the store."

Katie had to go back to the car and ask the boys to return the items she had just given them. It was a very humiliating experience, but she got all the items back, and we drove back to the store. Katie and Dottie went on inside to talk to the proprietor and tell her what Katie had done. Katie put all the merchandise on the counter and asked the woman for her forgiveness.

The whole experience was very embarrassing for Katie, but, fortunately, the proprietor was very warm and loving, and she spent quite a bit of time talking to Katie, telling her how much she appreciated her honesty.

Later, Dottie took Katie aside and told her a story about a time when she was only six years old and had gone to the store with her mother. On the way out, she had taken some gum, and when her mother discovered it later, she made Dottie go back to the store and do the same thing Katie had just done—return the merchandise and apologize. It was a great opportunity to let Katie know that her parents are human, too, and they knew how she felt.

You Are Not Responsible for Your Kids

Whenever I have to hold my children accountable, I try to teach them the principles of servant leadership that Jesus taught His disciples. In Philippians 2:5–10 (the *kenosis* passage), Paul speaks of how Jesus emptied Himself of His divine attributes so He could become a servant, made in human likeness. Despite all the power at His command, Jesus always taught and ministered as a servant-leader, never as an autocratic dictator.

For example, as Jesus and the twelve were going to Jerusalem for that final time, the apostles got in a wrangle over who was the greatest. Once more, with infinite patience, the Lord taught them that " . . . whoever wants to become great among you must be your servant, and whoever wants to be first must be your slave . . ." (Matthew 20:26–27, NIV).

Jesus never ruled over His followers, and He never became responsible *for them*. Instead, He was the servant-leader who was responsible *to them,* always teaching them by word and example what they needed to know.

Whenever we are responsible for someone, we set them up for failure as well as ourselves. Always remember that you are not responsible *for* your children. When I say that in parent seminars, some people bristle because I have just threatened their very purpose for being a parent. But then I go on to explain that no parent can stop a child, even a small child, from having a temper tantrum, for example. You might gag the child, or restrain the child in some other way, but the temper tantrum is still going on inside.

As the child grows older, and you try to teach him more and more about responsibility, you have to trust that he will learn and take that responsibility by his own free choice. The law may say you are responsible for your child's actions, but in the final analysis, your child must become a responsible, accountable human being on his own.

What does it mean specifically to be responsible to your children? I am responsible to love them and love their mother. I am responsible to provide them with food, shelter, and clothing.

I am responsible to educate them, to take them to church and youth group. I am responsible to hug them and tell them often, "I love you." I am responsible to listen to them and be available to them, and to do things with them.

But I am really not responsible *for* them. Ultimately, what they do with their lives—the choices they make—is their responsibility, not mine.

The Great Kindergarten "Prison Break"

Being responsible to my kids and following through to make them accountable is something I have to work at because there is an art to doing it lovingly but firmly. Dottie recalls that her mother had a gift for correcting her children without squelching who they were—their uniqueness. Four-year-old Heather loves to hear Dottie tell about the time she was in kindergarten and led her entire class in "the great nap-time prison break." Kindergarten was a lot of fun for Dottie, except for nap time, which she hated because she was so hyperactive.

One day Dottie decided to liven things up a little. She organized her class of thirty children, and when the teacher wasn't looking, Dottie gave the signal. All the kids jumped off their mats and ran out the door, down the street, and through the woods to Dottie's house, several blocks away.

The frantic teacher came huffing and puffing in hot pursuit, trying to catch up to her little charges, but they all arrived in Dottie's backyard laughing and shouting. A very excited group of little kindergartners thought that nap time had turned into just about the best time they ever had!

Dottie's mother heard the commotion and came running out to the backyard. When the teacher told Dottie's mother what had happened, she was very sympathetic because she could see the teacher was extremely worried as well as very tired from chasing her thirty kindergartners down the street. She helped herd Dottie and the rest of the kids to class, and assured the teacher that she would talk to Dottie about never having this kind of thing happen again.

Later, when Dottie got home from kindergarten, she and her mom sat down and talked about what had happened. Dottie remembers the scene this way:

> My mom didn't spank me or put me on restriction for three weeks. She didn't take television away, or anything like that. Instead of clobbering me, what I remember is that she encouraged my leadership ability and shared in what I was feeling as she helped me sort out what kinds of behavior aren't acceptable.
>
> My mom made it clear that there are certain things you just don't do, and I remember very clearly telling her that I'd never do it again, but at the same time she brought out a lot of positive things—my leadership and creativity, for example—and she didn't knock all the excitement and fun out of what had happened.
>
> My mother had a tremendous balance for enforcing the limits with plenty of love. She was a real role model to me in this regard. Frankly, none of my children has ever done anything quite that "creative," but

if they ever do, I'm not at all sure I could react quite as calmly and as warmly as my mother did.

In basic personality, I'm much more like my dad, who would sometimes lose his temper with us but always came back later to apologize.

I appreciate Dottie's honesty concerning how she might respond if Heather, for example, led twenty-nine of her kindergarten classmates in a "prison break." I know my own reaction wouldn't be very calm. As I shared in chapter 3, I always have to fight the "come down too hard urge" when I discipline the kids.

Sometimes I'll ground them for several weeks, and in rare cases even several months. When this happens, Dottie steps in to help. All she says is, "Honey, I think the discipline may be a little too hard for what really happened."

My wife never jumps all over me and says, "You can't do that." Instead, she'll say, "Josh, I'll leave it up to you, but I think your penalty is too strong."

Almost invariably I will reply, "Well, what do you think it ought to be?"

Then we discuss it and reset a more reasonable form of discipline. After that, I go to the children, confess I was too severe, and, if an apology is warranted, I ask their forgiveness.

One reason I'm sharing some of these revelations about the McDowell household with you is to make it clear that we try hard not to be permissive parents. We try our best to show our kids love by accepting and appreciating them, but we also balance that love with limits. In fact, our limits are part of our love for them and they know it.

What we are trying to do as we teach our kids to be accountable is help them develop the self-discipline they need to live an effective, useful, and happy life. So often I run across stories about great athletes, or people with other great talent or ability, who fail because they are not self-disciplined. The only way a child can learn self-discipline is to be disciplined first by his parents. And as someone has said:

If you don't have enough willpower to submit to somebody else, you'll never have enough willpower to submit to yourself.

Being Accountable Takes Humility—and Patience

My main goal in this chapter is to suggest some ways you might want to try being accountable to your kids. But let me warn you, it takes humility to be accountable—and patience. One of the features of our "Be a Hero" video series is to open each segment with a brief skit in which professional actors play the "Preston Family." Mom and Dad Preston's trials and tribulations with their three children give Dick and me excellent material to kick off our discussion for each program concerning what it means to be a hero.

Dad Preston, in particular, has a difficult time relating to his fifteen-year-old son, Nathan, but eventually both parents discover the need to work more on their relationship to their kids and less on enforcing their rules. In the final scene, Dad calls a family conference and hands sealed letters to all of the children. Mom's letter to Heather, the oldest at seventeen, says:

> I love you. I love your sensitivity, your honesty, your spirit, and caring heart. This note gives you permission to remind me when I'm not sensitive, honest, or caring. I'm sorry for all those times I've been angry and impatient with you. I want so much to be a better mother and friend to you.
>
> Your Mom

Dad's letter to Heather also expresses his love and pride in her, and then he goes on to say:

> This note gives you permission to tell me when you think I'm making decisions for you rather than *with* you. Use it whenever you need it, and when it wears out, I promise to write you another one.

Next to read her letters is the youngest child, eleven-year-old Ashley. In his letter to Ashley, Dad confesses being too busy and says:

> Forgive me for not giving you more of my time. I really want to be at every soccer game next year. This note gives you permission to remind me when I get too busy with other things. Please use it.

Nathan reads his letters last. His mother writes:

> I love you, Nathan Allen. You are the second man in my life. Please hand me this note when I forget to watch you be the man you are becoming.

Finally, Nathan reads Dad's note, which is a request for forgiveness:

Dear Nate,

Please forgive me for trying to live my life out in you. Playing sports I never played. Making grades I never made. Being better than I ever was. Forgive me for my unkind words and my harsh spirit. This note gives you permission to tell me to back off and give you some breathing room. I need you to help me be a more patient father. I pray for you every day. I do love you more than I can express.

Your Dad

I'm including these letters from our video sound track to suggest still more ways you might want to let your kids know you're willing to be accountable. Maybe you owe one or more of your children a note like one of those.

The father of the Preston family started out by making a typical error, using his authority without backing it up from his own life. Fortunately, he learned in time that authority is something to be used gently and lovingly instead of harshly and impatiently.

Have you ever thought about the kind of authority you display to your children? On what is your authority based and how do you use it? In the next chapter, Dick Day will look more closely at the final "A" in our Positive Parenting Plan.

To Think About, Discuss, or Try for Yourself

1.   According to this chapter, the best way to teach your children to be responsible and accountable is to be accountable to them. Do you agree or disagree? Talk with your spouse about how accountable you are to the children.

2.   Have you ever sat down with your children and told them you want to be accountable to them? For example: "I want to be accountable to you, as your dad (or mom); I want you to tell me whenever I'm not living by the rules or when I'm not being fair."

3.   One reason Josh wants to be accountable to his wife and children is that he realizes "good intentions don't automatically become reality." Why does this seem to be true with so many people? We all have good intentions, but why don't they become reality? Would being held accountable help good intentions become reality in your family? Why or why not?

4.   Do you agree with the author that a strong leader is the one who is willing to be criticized and held to account? What characteristics does a strong leader of a family have? How would you rate yourself on a scale of 1 to 10—10 being "very strong"?

5.   According to this chapter, why is it important to be responsible to your children, but not *for* your children? Can you think of ways you and your spouse may be falling into the trap of being responsible *for* your children? How can you correct this drift if it is there?

6.   Toward the end of this chapter, Josh includes several notes from parents, letting their children know they want to be accountable to them. Could you adapt any of these notes for use with your children?

7.   Fathers, read again Matthew 20:26–27, where Jesus talks about serving others. Is this passage indicative of your role as a father in your home?

14

How Not to Drive Your Kids Crazy—or Worse

(*Dick Day*)

How were you parented? That is, what style did your parents use? The answer to this question will tell you a lot about your own attitude toward parental authority—what it is and how it should be used.

As the charts on page 190 show, there are four parenting styles that can be found in most homes:

- Autocratic—"You'll do it my way, or else!"
- Permissive—"You can do anything you want."
- Neglectful—"I really don't care what you do."
- Relational—"I'm listening . . . I care about you . . . I want to understand . . . This time we'll do it this way because. . . ."

Autocrats Wield Absolute Power

Each of these styles reveals a certain attitude toward the use of authority by the parent. The autocratic parent is an "absolute ruler," whom Webster defines at three levels. First, there is the dictator who "holds and exercises absolute power." At a slightly less ominous level, the autocrat is one who is "invested with or assumes absolute independent power over others." At the very least, an autocrat is any "domineering self-willed person."

As the diagram on page 190 shows, when autocratic parents wield absolute power over children, they are too strong on control and too weak on support. *Limits* overpower and outweigh *Love.*

In some homes, autocratic parenting can take terrible twists and result in tragic child abuse of the worst kind. Every now and then the newspapers will carry a story of a child who has been beaten, starved, and even locked up—sometimes for years.

In one case I read about recently, police, acting on a tip from a child abuse hotline, confronted the parents of seven children and discovered a malnourished, twelve-year-old girl locked in a four-by-five-foot closet. The floor was covered with human waste, fast food wrappers, and cockroaches. The child, who had the physical development of a seven-year-old, had on a tattered sweat suit, soaked with urine. Her face had bruises from frequent beatings.

Further investigation revealed that the little girl had been locked in the closet for at least a month and she had endured this kind of periodic treatment for the past ten years. Apparently, her six brothers and sisters had not been treated as badly, but one of the officers who discovered the girl said he had seen hundreds of child abuse cases, but "never anything like this."[1]

Obviously, this kind of "absolute control" approach to parenting is bizarre and even unbelievable. These parents are an extreme example of autocratic behavior, but there are many lesser variations that do tremendous damage to many children.

Autocratics Often Provide "Good" Homes

Many autocratic parents give children "good homes." They feed and clothe them well, let them play with other children, and in short, seem to provide everything needed for a "normal" life. Everything but enough support and love.

While they would never beat their children or lock them in closets, autocratic parents still reign as absolute rulers of their families. They are very big on rules, but low on relationships.

Living in an autocracy causes children to react in one of two ways: flight or fight. When children choose *flight,* they typically withdraw and learn to go along and "be obedient"—on the surface. Inside, however, they are seething. Dr. Howard Hendricks, Professor of Christian Education at Dallas Theological Seminary, often tells

What is Your Parenting Style?

Autocratic: Strong control but little support

Permissive: Strong support but little control

Indifferent: Little or no control, little or no support, the child feels like a non-entity

Relational (authoritative): Correct balance of control and support

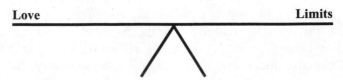

the story of the child whose father told him to sit down. The child didn't want to sit down and the father thundered, *"Sit down or I'll make you sit down!"*

The child sat down, but under his breath he muttered, "I may be sitting down on the outside, but on the inside I'm *standing up!"*

In other variations of flight, children can crumble and will take desperate measures because they can't take it anymore. In these cases children may become runaways and, in the worst possible scenarios, suicides.

When a child chooses to *fight,* his anger is out in the open. He complains, talks back, and even lashes out verbally and physically. In short, the child rebels because the rules he must live under are not cushioned or filtered by a loving relationship with his parents.

When I was involved in marriage and family counseling, I often had to deal with autocratic parents who would finally come to me in desperation and say, "I don't know what to do with my kid. He's all over the place—won't obey, won't do his schoolwork, won't come home on time. I'm at my wits' end."

"Well," I would ask, "what are you doing?"

"Why, I'm grounding him, of course. No television, no allowance, no car keys. When I say grounded, I mean *grounded!"*

Now I always made it a policy never to tell parents what to do with their children, but in cases like this, I always had the same suggestion:

"Would you be willing to let up on your rules and punishments and try working on your relationship with your child?"

"Let up on the rules? You don't know my kid. He'll go berserk!"

My next question was always, "Well, is your plan working?"

Most parents got my point. Obviously, their plan wasn't working or they wouldn't be in my office paying me to tell me their troubles and get some advice. Some of them would even take my suggestions and occasionally be able to change their ways. Many, however, did not. It's hard for autocrats to change. Their "absolute power" is just too important and they are too insecure to let go.

The Other Extreme Is Permissiveness

The other end of the spectrum is the permissive parent who is strong on support but a wimp on control. As the diagram illustrates, *Love* overpowers *Limits* and, again, there is a serious imbalance in the family environment. You have probably heard about or seen permissive parents in action. Actually, the child is the one in action, while the parents sort of stand and watch him destroy flower beds, furniture, and the peace of the household, in general.

Permissively-parented kids often hold their parents hostage. They may refuse to take naps, resorting to temper tantrums, screaming until their poor mother is willing to grant them any wish to keep them quiet. Perhaps the little tyrant wants a glass of water, so mother runs frantically to get one. But when she brings it, he pushes it violently aside because she wasn't fast enough.

Mother stands there, offering the glass of water and warning her son, "If you don't drink it by the time I count to five, I'm taking it away."

Naturally, the count of five comes and goes and the child still hasn't taken the water. But as his mother walks away, the child screams again for a drink. Around and around the parent and child go, with the child in charge because the parent will not set limits and the child knows it.

Permissively-parented children get their way a lot, but they are no happier than the children in the autocratic homes because the balance of *Love* and *Limits* is not there. Frankly, the lack of limits causes the child to think: "If they really cared about me, they'd be more interested in what I do . . . they would say no sometimes . . . I guess they don't really love me."

The Permissive Generation Produced the Indifferent Generation

In 1970, a young unknown psychologist rocked the parenting and publishing world with a book entitled, *Dare to Discipline*. Dr. James Dobson's message was, "It's okay to discipline your kids within a framework of love and affection. Children need to be taught self-discipline and responsible behavior, and it's okay to set limits."[2]

Dare to Discipline was a direct response to the permissive approach to parenting that had swept much of the nation, beginning with publications such as Dr. Benjamin Spock's book, *Baby and Child Care*. But permissive parenting didn't start because of the advice of a book or two. Parents who were permissive in the forties, fifties, and sixties came out of a Depression background. They had also gone through World War II, when they had to go without a lot of things, even though there might have been money to buy them.

When better times rolled in the 1950s, these parents vowed that they'd give their children everything they didn't have. In fact, they proceeded to have an extraordinary number of children, creating what is now called the "baby boom," which occurred between 1946 and 1964. These parents of baby boom children became, in many respects, indulgent.

It is no surprise that an indulged child is likely to become a self-indulgent adult. These children of the baby boom, the so-called "Me generation," became parents themselves—and in many cases slipped into certain modes of indifferent parenting. In some homes, this indifference is glaringly evident, but in other families it's hard to spot.

Throughout the eighties and into the nineties, the media has been full of the "have it all" propaganda—careers, children, the big house, the BMW. Many parents have been caught up in this concept of success and have tried to keep up too fast a pace. As a result, family life has suffered and, without meaning to, some parents have had so little time for their children that their lack of interest can be interpreted as indifference.

I am not trying to make a wholesale indictment of the entire baby boomer generation of parents. Many baby boomer parents are involved with their children, and are doing a good job. Nonetheless, the pattern is there. If you are a baby boomer parent who was raised somewhat indulgently, you might do well to reread the chapters on availability and come to grips with just how much time you have for your children and your spouse.

Be aware that it is entirely possible to provide a nice home, buy the kids all the yuppie goodies, and still be unavailable physically and/or emotionally. Indifference can be communicated in very subtle ways. And when children feel they are being parented indifferently, they can become hurt and angry. Indeed, perhaps our next generation will be the "hurt and angry generation" who will continue the pattern of dysfunction when they grow up, marry, and have children of their own.

I know from personal experience how the pattern of dysfunction can occur. I grew up in a home where my parents had divorced, but later remarried. Due to the pressures of my dad's job as an executive vice-president, he and my mother moved in fast social circles where drinking was expected. Eventually, they became "functioning alcoholics."

I knew my parents loved me, but they were so wrapped up in their own lives that they paid me little attention. To cope with my life at home, I withdrew—spending most of my time in my room listening to my radio, but tuned out on everything and everyone else, particularly studying. My family was so dysfunctional, I went through two semesters of my freshman year in high school with straight F's. Yet no one—teachers or parents—seemed interested.

Finally, toward the end of my second term, my parents stopped long enough between cocktail parties to realize that they hadn't seen my report card all year long. When they did see it, they tried to take what they thought was "loving action"; the next year I was shipped off to a prep school to repeat my freshman grade.

I was well into my twenties, married, and with four small children when God intervened to save me and my family what undoubtedly would have been a continuance of the cycle of dysfunctionalism. When Charlotte and I became Christians, we vowed that the patterns of neglect that I'd known as a child would never be repeated—and they haven't.

The Balanced Approach Is Relational

In order to have the proper balance of *Love* and *Limits* (support and control), parents need the relational (authoritative) approach. As the diagram shows, there is an equal amount of love and limits resulting in a balanced relationship between parent and children. The children feel love but they also feel control, which adds to their security rather than taking it away.

It is no surprise that the relational approach to authoritative parenting features acceptance, appreciation, affection, and availability. To paraphrase a well-known passage in the book of James, the relational parent is "quick to listen, slow to judge and condemn, and even slower to become angry" (see James 1:21). At the same time, the relational parent is authoritative. This means holding the children accountable (while being accountable to the children yourself) and using authority lovingly and fairly.

We have devoted the greater part of this book to explaining why you must build your relationship to your children on love, but if that love is to be genuine and nurturing, you can never forget limits. Limits are the parameters in which the child can operate safely and securely. Proper limits allow the child to experiment, grow, and develop. Without these parameters of parental authority, the child has no solid basis on which to make sound decisions. Without parameters, there is only confusion and chaos.

When Josh and I speak of authority, we mean the God-given parameters that are found in His Word. God gave the Law, and He also gave the liberating love of Christ. Truth—God's truth—encircles the Christian believer and his or her family. God's truth does not entrap us; instead, it sets us free.

By its very nature, however, truth does have limits. Truth includes boundaries—fences, if you please. Without these fences, you don't have truth. You have a free-for-all, and anything goes.

Fenced Pastures Are Good for Sheep—and Kids

One day I was out for a walk on the mountainside and came across a man who was traveling the United States in a covered wagon. He had stopped to graze his mules on a meadow near Julian and I struck up a conversation with him. It turned out that he was very experienced in raising animals, and I happened to ask, "What's the best environment for raising livestock here, like your mules? Open grazing land, a large fenced pasture, or a corral?"

Without hesitation, he answered, "Oh, the fenced pasture, by far."

"Why?"

"Because when animals get into that open grazing land, they get lost. Often they may be attacked by predators. Open grazing land is just too unsafe. And, if you put them into a corral, they always have to be provided for. They can't roam around and provide for themselves. But when you put them into a good fenced pasture, all that they need is right there and they can still operate on their own."

After the man hitched up his mules and his covered wagon creaked on down the highway, I thought about our conversation and the fantastic analogy it suggests from Scripture. God has given us all we need in green pastures and still waters (see Psalm 23). And yet He has also given us fences—His perfect law of liberty and the truth that makes us free in Christ (see James 1:25, John 8:32). Fenced pastures are not only good for livestock; they make sense for how we parent our children as well, particularly in a culture that emphasizes relative thinking and the "anything goes" philosophy.

That's why there must be parameters—absolutes that give stability and authority in the child's life. At the same time, there must be balance. One study of adolescent/parent relationships revealed that children reared under autocratic control are likely to have the following characteristics: hostility toward parents; prejudice toward older people; anti-social activities, such as stealing, lying, fighting, and vandalism; feelings of social alienation; rejection of traditional moral standards; and inability to relate well to people.

At the other end of the spectrum, we have the child who was reared permissively. This produces adolescents who assume little responsibility for their behavior. Few of them are likely to go out of their way to help people, by doing such things as coaching a fellow student with homework, mowing a lawn for an older person who could not do it himself, or running an errand for a shut-in.

Permissively-raised adolescents are less likely to want to live by the moral standards of their parents. They are more likely to become involved in stealing, lying, drinking, and self-indulgent behavior, which includes the use and abuse of alcohol, sex, and drugs. They are more likely to seek out films that are sexually explicit and erotic. In short, permissiveness encourages a hedonistic and anti-social lifestyle that has tragedy built into it everywhere.

Clearly then, a child needs firm limits, but those limits have to be built upon love—the acceptance and appreciation described in earlier chapters.

How to Recognize a Relational Parent

We have looked at three different parenting styles we want to avoid: autocratic, permissive, and indifferent. But what about the relational authoritative parent—the ideal that we hope to reach? What does a relational parent look like? More importantly, what does the relational parent do while providing loving authority?

Volumes have been written on how to be an effective authoritative parent. One expert emphasizes one thing; a second expert contradicts the first. I have found no better description of the relational parent than a verse from one of Paul's letters which says: "And, fathers, do not provoke your children to anger; bring them up in the discipline and instruction of the Lord" (Ephesians 6:4, NASB).

What did Paul mean by "provoke your children to anger"? The *New International Version* says, "Fathers, do not *exasperate* your children . . ." J. B. Phillips translates this verse, "Fathers, don't *over-correct* your children or make it difficult for them to obey the commandment." And *The Living Bible* says: "Don't keep on *scolding and nagging* your children, making them angry and resentful" (italics mine).

With the different negative parenting styles in mind, one way to paraphrase Ephesians 6:4 could be, "Do not drive your children crazy with autocratic, permissive, or indifferent parenting. But, instead, build a loving, authoritative relationship, based on the parameters of God's Word."

Or, to paraphrase it even more simply, we can review what was stated so clearly back in chapter 3:

Rules without relationship lead to rebellion.

So far so good, but how are we to do what Paul suggests in the second part of Ephesians 6:4, " . . . bring them up in the training and instruction of the Lord"? When "push comes to shove," how do relational, authoritative parents discipline their children? Following are some basic principles:

Make the Payoff for Misbehavior Small

It helps to remember that when children do something wrong, they are usually seeking attention. Now obviously, you cannot ignore your child when he or she misbehaves. You have to deal with it, but the question is *how* do you deal with it? What does the child see and hear as you respond to his misbehavior?

If the child can get the volume of your voice to go up, if he can get you red in the face, if he can provoke you in any number of ways, he will conclude that misbehavior is the best way to get your attention.

On the other hand, if you can deal with his misbehavior quietly, without long loud lectures, or other angry outbursts, the payoff will not be nearly as big. One simple approach is to quietly tell the child that this kind of thing won't be tolerated and, if necessary, separate him from the rest of the family for awhile. Remember, it's harder to get attention when you're all alone. The "chair in the corner" may seem like an old-fashioned idea, but with many children it is extremely effective.

I realize that with some children it isn't that simple, but however you deal with your child's misbehavior, keep in mind that children are bound to do some things wrong. They are bound to misbehave on occasion simply because they are children. Make it your goal not to make such a big issue out of their negative behavior; instead, try to accentuate their positive behavior. As you learned in chapter 7, try to catch them doing something right instead of always looking for what they are doing wrong. To put it in the terms of the old popular song, try to "accentuate the positive and eliminate the negative."

TYPES OF AUTHORITY

AUTOCRATIC　　　　**POSITION and POWER**

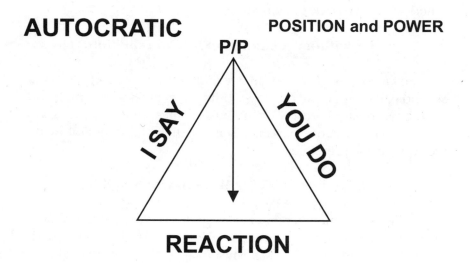

REACTION

RELATIONAL

RESPONSE

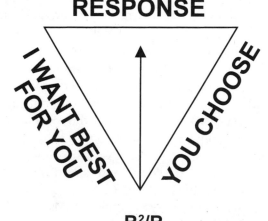

R²/R

**RESPONSIBLE TO
OUT OF A
RELATIONSHIP**

To do this effectively, you need a system of discipline that gives the child every chance to learn and to mature. I believe that Scripture teaches two modes of positive discipline that psychologists have "discovered" only in recent times. One is called "natural consequences," and the other, "logical consequences." Both are based on simple cause and effect principles.

The Prodigal Son Suffered Natural Consequences

The parable of the Prodigal Son is an excellent illustration of natural consequences. The young man decided to leave home and live it up, and he demanded that his father give him his share of the inheritance. The father knew what would happen, but he handed the money over anyway, and let the boy go and learn character development the hard way.

Natural consequences took their toll and eventually the young prodigal wound up eating with the pigs because that was all he had. The key line in the entire parable is, "When he came to his senses . . . " (Luke 15:17, NIV). It took natural consequences to bring the boy to his senses. He decided to return home to his father where he was accepted and loved more than ever (see Luke 15:11–32).

It is interesting that the father not only let him go, but gave him his inheritance. Many a father may let his son go, but how many would give him an inheritance to just throw away? No way! The father of the prodigal, however, was more than willing. He placed the development of moral character above financial security. All too often in our society, our major concern is financial rather than character development. As parents, we need to ask ourselves what values we are communicating to our children as important.

I recall using natural consequences to teach Jonathan an important lesson when he was very small. We had an open fireplace in our home that was at floor level, and I often worried about Jonathan. Not realizing what fire could do, he could reach into the fireplace and get terribly burned while Charlotte and I weren't looking.

One evening we were sitting at dinner eating by candlelight. Jonathan started to reach up to touch the candle flame and Charlotte started to stop him, but I said, "No, let him do it."

Jonathan stuck his finger in the flame and withdrew it immediately with a cry of pain. He wasn't burned badly, but he was burned just enough to learn the power of fire and to respect it. Some people might say it was cruel to let Jonathan stick his finger into the candle flame, but I don't think so. I'd much rather have him learn that fire burns from a tiny flame than from a roaring blaze. From then on, little Jonathan respected fire and my fears of his getting near the fireplace were greatly diminished.

Logical Consequences Are Set Beforehand

The other mode of discipline described in Scripture is logical consequences. This simply means that the parent determines with the child that certain consequences will happen if the child does not fulfill his responsibilities or misbehaves in some way. For example, "If you don't eat all your dinner, you get no dessert," or "If you don't feed your puppy, you don't eat either."

We see the precedent for logical consequences taking place in the Garden with Adam and Eve. God laid everything out for them and then made it clear that the one tree they could not eat from was the Tree of the Knowledge of Good and Evil. If they did eat from that tree, the logical consequence would be that they would "surely die" (see Genesis 2:15–17).

Tempted by the serpent, Eve ate from the tree, and then Adam followed suit. When God discovered what had happened, the consequences came swiftly. Adam and Eve became susceptible to physical death, and all its related penalties, such as pain in childbirth, living by the sweat of one's brow, and banishment from Paradise itself (see Genesis 3:1–19).

God had spelled out the boundaries in which Adam and Eve could operate, and when they chose to violate or to cross those boundaries, they had to face the consequences. Yet God did not set these limits until He had first demonstrated His love by providing for their every need—physically, emotionally, rationally, socially, sexually, and spiritually. When He set limits, God was giving Adam and Eve an opportunity to respond to His love by trusting and obeying.

Parenting children works much the same way. Parents are responsible to spell out the boundaries for their children. These are the limits that you build upon the loving foundation you have already established. By laying down limits, you make the child accountable for his actions and behavior.

Sticking to Your Guns Is Crucial

In chapter 13, Josh described how badly he felt when Sean trudged out of that school yard to go back home and take care of his responsibilities, *but Josh stuck to his guns,* a critical part of using logical consequences. He knew that he couldn't help his son learn responsibility and develop character by letting him slough off on what he had promised to do. Taking out the garbage for him, or even being a "good guy" and letting him do it after school would not teach Sean what he really needed to learn.

When my oldest son, Dick, got his driver's license, he and I agreed that if he got any moving violations, he would pay the fine and lose his driving privileges for thirty days. I can still remember the day Dick got his first moving violation. He came in timidly and said, "Dad, I got a ticket."

I don't know what Dick expected, but all I said was, "Where are the car keys?"

Dick handed me the keys. He also paid the fine, and he didn't drive the car for thirty days. There was no lecture. There was no asking him to explain, "Why did you do that?" The logical consequences had already been spelled out and Dick knew that he was paying a price he had already agreed upon.

Forgive—and Ask for Forgiveness

In the situations I describe above, everything came out okay as logical consequences were enforced. Every parent knows, however, that there are times when it doesn't always end that well or that smoothly. There are times when tempers flare, words are said, and family life can get very sticky. The parent who wants to be a hero must always be ready to forgive, as well as always be prepared to ask for forgiveness.

Four of the hardest words any of us can ever utter are "Will you forgive me?" Nonetheless, they are words you must learn to use often if you are genuinely intent on being accountable to your children and your spouse, always trying to use authority as a loving parameter, not a club.

On one occasion our oldest son, Dick, and his family were visiting us while they were on leave from serving overseas. As their time with us drew to an end, we decided to go over to a nearby state park for a big family picnic and going-away party. Charlotte packed a beautiful picnic lunch, Dick and his wife, Betty, gathered up their kids, and we all left for the park.

It should have been a great day, but there was a problem. A very old and dear friend of Charlotte's had phoned her a few hours before to tell her that she had recently learned she had cancer and that she was coming out to San Diego for treatment. She asked Charlotte if she could come down from Julian to San Diego to meet her plane and take her over to the clinic to get her settled.

Charlotte was torn in two directions: she wanted to support her dear friend, but on the other hand, she also wanted to be with her children and grandchildren at our very special going-away party.

After we got to the park and set everything up, Charlotte stayed as long as she could, but soon the time approached when she had to leave. I was sitting at a picnic table with her and said something to which she didn't respond. I asked her again, and she still didn't answer. I asked her a third time, raising my voice to get her attention. I got it all right. She turned around and snapped, "Why are you yelling at me?"

"What do you mean, yelling at you? I asked you twice and you didn't answer. Why are you so tuned out?"

I should have realized why Charlotte was so "tuned out." She was thinking about going down to see her friend, and her mind was definitely somewhere else. She was also tense because she had to leave the family gathering where she really preferred to be. And maybe I was a little tense, too, because she was going to miss the rest of our special family day with all of us together.

The Domino Effect Got Everybody Upset

A few minutes later, as Charlotte drove away, there was a tension in the air that you could cut with a knife. Dick and his wife, Betty, noticed it, too. In fact, the whole episode created a strange domino effect. In a matter of minutes, Dick and Betty were having words with each other, and then their kids started to bicker and argue as well. Of course, Dick and Betty had to get on the kids and it went round and round.

The whole thing was much like the scenario where the boss yells at his employee, the man comes home and yells at his wife, the wife yells at the kids, the kids yell at the dog, and the dog chases the cat!

As I thought about it, I began to understand what had happened. I had reacted to being treated in what I thought was an indifferent manner because Charlotte hadn't responded to me. When I realized why she had been so tuned out, I knew that what I had done was wrong. As soon as I saw her again I would ask her to forgive me.

Charlotte got back late that night and it turned out she'd gone through a similar process. As she had started down the road and started thinking about what had happened, she saw how silly the whole thing was. Then she'd gotten a flat tire and had even more time to reflect upon it while a service station attendant repaired it.

When Charlotte walked in, we were all sitting in the living room and the first thing on my mind was asking her to forgive me. Asking for my forgiveness was the first thing on her mind, as well, and there we were, virtually stumbling over each other trying to ask for forgiveness. That caused another chain reaction with the family, this time a positive one. Dick and Betty started to ask each other for forgiveness, and even the kids joined in.

The Power of "Will You Forgive Me?"

Later, we all sat down as a family and laughed together about what had taken place and what we had learned from it. I realize this little story doesn't have a lot to do with discipline or logical consequences, but it does illustrate what can happen when sharp words are exchanged. "Will you forgive me?" is the soft answer that can turn away anger and make things right (Proverbs 15:1). There will be many times as you discipline your child when both of you may need to use those words.

Keep in mind that there is a vast difference between saying, "I'm sorry," and saying, "Will you forgive me?" The words, "I'm sorry," involve one person. But when you say, "Will you forgive me?" you are involving two or more people. The phrase, "Will you forgive me?" is relational. It builds the relationship because it demands an answer by the other person.

I admit there is also a risk to asking, "Will you forgive me?" You make yourself vulnerable when you ask for forgiveness and the other person may just turn around and say, "No, I won't forgive you." Your own child might do that very thing out of immature anger or not really understanding what's going on. But it's a risk you have to take, because it role-models the kind of vulnerability you want your child to learn.

Small children will often be willing to say, "I'm sorry . . . I'm sorry . . . I'm sorry," when they are disciplined, but if you ask them to go up to someone else and say, "Will you forgive me?" they'll squirm. Start teaching them at a young age that being sorry is good, but being willing to ask for forgiveness is much better.

In Tense Situations, Do a Magnet Check

When I start feeling tension with my children, I find that it's best to try to step back and see them as God sees them—persons of infinite worth. This helps put me in a mode of acceptance even when the situation may call for discipline. I can still affirm them as I deal with their behavior.

I call this stepping back a "magnet check." When two magnets are separated and not in the same magnetic field, they have no influence on each other. If you place the two magnets within the same magnetic field, they will do one of two things: become attracted to each other or push away from each other.

Our human emotions make us very much like magnets. You don't have magnetic powers, but you do have emotions and so does your child. Living together in a family puts you and your children into the same "emotional field," and when that happens, there is a result similar to placing magnets close to one another. One of two things happens: you either come together with your child or you react to each other and push each other away.

Whenever I find myself in a tense situation with my children, I ask myself some hard questions: "Why is our relationship under stress? Why am I reacting to my child? Why is my child reacting to me?" When things get tense, or worse, in your family, you can count on it: somebody's security is being threatened and your acceptance of the child is also in jeopardy.

Be aware that doing magnet checks is your responsibility, not the child's. As an adult, you are the one who should be able to step back—outside the situation—and be able to see what's happening. Then you can bring any anger you may have under control. And, if necessary, you can ask forgiveness.

Doing magnet checks always helps me deal with the situation. The magnet check makes it possible to always accept and affirm my children, while at the same time invoking limits, if necessary. Acceptance and affirmation, balanced by limits, is what nurture is all about. It also works with one's mate or in any other relationship where people come into the same emotional field.

Parents Who Have Ears, Please Hear

While doing family counseling, I had a thirteen-year-old girl and her parents come to see me. The father was in a high-profile

EMOTIONS

EMOTIONS are like magnets—

In different field they aren't affected.

In same field they will either,

REACT

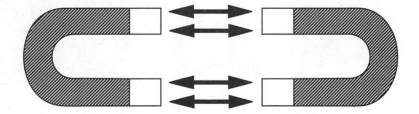

or
RESPOND

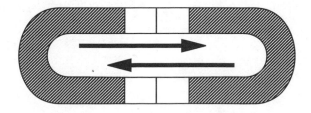

Christian music ministry and traveled the country singing and giving his testimony.

As we talked, I made some observations that set the father off and he proceeded to give a beautiful theological dissertation—something very doctrinally sound about what the Bible says concerning the family. It was a beautiful job, well calculated to impress me and intimidate his wife and daughter. But Dad had obviously never heard Josh McDowell say, "You can con a con, you can fool a fool, but you can't kid a kid."

When the father finished, the daughter turned to her dad and in a quiet, almost wistful voice, she said: "Dad, I wish you could have heard what you just said and do it."

This girl was not rebellious or disrespectful. She desperately wanted her family to be together, but her dad never could hear her. He was too intent on keeping his power and what he believed was "authority." His daughter was telling him that the real secret to authority is a servant's heart. The servant-leader listens to his family and is always more concerned about relationships than rules. To be a servant-leader, however, the one in authority must know what it is to be loved, to have both a sense of security and significance because he or she is accepted and appreciated—beginning with God's grace.

The greatest servant-leader of them all said on several occasions: "He who has ears to hear, let him hear." Relational parents hear and then do. In the final analysis, that's how to be a hero to your kids!

You can identify the difference between the autocratic leader and the relational servant-leader from the chart on page 190. You will also notice the emotional results from each on page 205. What kind of leadership did your parents model? What kind of parent are you? What kind of parent do you wish to be?

To Think About, Discuss, or Try for Yourself

1.   According to this chapter, there are four styles of parenting: autocratic, permissive, neglectful, and relational (authoritative). Which styles operate in your home? Which parent uses what style the most and why?

2.   Why is it possible to provide a "good home" and still have a basically autocratic style of parenting?

3.   Why are permissively-parented children no happier than those with autocratic parents?

4.   In this chapter, Dick mentions that it's possible to provide a nice home with all the "goodies" and still be unavailable physically or emotionally to your children. Do you see even a remote danger of this in your own family? Talk with your spouse about how you can correct this kind of drift.

5.   Take out a sheet of paper and make a brief list of the characteristics of a relational (authoritative) parent. Which of these characteristics are true of you? Which would you like to be able to do better?

6.   Do you ever use natural or logical consequences with your children? Think of some examples. If you would like to start using logical consequences, start slowly in little ways and always stick to your guns when the logical consequences must be enforced.

7.   According to the author, what are four of the hardest words a parent would ever have to say? How good are you at asking forgiveness? How would your other family members rate you as being able to forgive and being willing to ask forgiveness when it is needed?

8.   Next time you face a tense situation, try doing the "magnet check" the author describes in this chapter. Remember, the key questions are: "Why is our relationship under stress right now? Why am I reacting to my child? And why is my child reacting to me?" Finally, "What can I do to change things?"

9.   Now that you have completed the Six A's of Positive Parenting—acceptance, appreciation, availability, affection, accountability, and authority—you may like to do a study, as an individual, as a couple, or as a family of these principles as found in the Bible. The four basic building blocks (availability and affection are demonstrations of acceptance and appreciation) are taught in the Book of Ephesians.

Acceptance by grace (Ephesians 1:1–3:21)

Appreciation by edification (see 4:1–5:20)

Accountability by submission (see 5:21–6:9)

Authority by God (see 6:10–6:20)

Note the verses that especially speak to you about these principles.

Final Thoughts

Never Stop Being a Hero!

As YOU'VE read this book, it has probably occurred to you several times, "There is really nothing complex or difficult here. This is all biblically-based, God-given common sense—the things that all of us as parents should be doing with and for our children."

Exactly.

As we said earlier, the Six A's for Positive Parenting contain no magic formula for success. What the Six A's do provide are some useful tools to be a parent in a culture that is essentially anti-family. It's a culture that teaches self-centeredness, greed, and violence. Its theme song is "I Gotta Be Me," and its perverted gospel claims that "all truth is relative."

As Dick and I have shared our thoughts and convictions about the Six A's, an old saying has kept coming to mind:

Heroes are made, not born

As a parent, I know that's all too true. And I also know that being a hero is a *long-term* process! The challenge to be accepting, appreciative, affectionate, and available is there every day. The responsibility to be accountable and relational is part of every waking moment, especially those moments when you're awakened in the night by anything from a plea for a drink of water to a call from the local police station. Even if you're a hero to your kids, there is no 100 percent guarantee that you won't have some problems—even rebellion. When you are a parent, no matter how good, problems come with the territory.

I Have a Special Hope for Dads

We hope, however, that you and your spouse will cope with the problems and challenges by adapting and applying the principles you've read in these pages. Or perhaps you've already been practicing some of these concepts, and you'll want to renew your commitment to keep on doing what you've already been doing to be positive parents. It's our special hope that some of you dads, in particular, will use at least some of the Six A's to make significant changes in how you relate to your family.

It's my guess that nothing could make your wife more joyful than hearing you say: "Would you help me learn to be more acceptant? Would you encourage me to work at catching the kids doing something *right*? Would you let me know when I'm getting too busy and too preoccupied? Will you help me be more accountable to my family?"

I'm even hoping that divorced single moms will encourage their former husbands by saying: "Please read this book. We both have a tremendous responsibility to the kids, and even though we don't live together any more, we both can still apply these principles to love and care for our kids."

Every day, dozens of voices trumpet from television sets, theater screens, radio loudspeakers, and even from some classrooms, delivering one basic message: "Don't listen to authority—don't pay attention to your parents." Few will deny that the task of parenting gets tougher every day. I believe that parents need to support and pull for each other. Talk to other moms and dads at work or in your church. Find out what they're doing, what they're facing, and how they feel. Watch other parents you believe are doing an effective job. Ask them questions—and listen to their answers.

If you consciously keep looking, you will find help. You will learn things that you can apply no matter what age your kids might be. Whether they're unsteady toddlers or confident cocksure teenagers, they still need positive parenting. They still need acceptance, appreciation, and all the rest.

Mr. Mom Rides Again—and Again

Wherever I go I try to tell groups of parents that I know their task is monumental, and that it can cover every possible kind of emergency and challenge. Just a few months ago, I was reminded of just how monumental that task can be—especially for mothers.

As a special and different birthday gift to Dottie, I offered to be Mr. Mom for ten days while she visited her parents, brother, and sister in Florida. Dottie was thrilled at the prospect because she really wanted to see her family and she needed the rest.

We agreed that three-year-old Heather would go with her to Florida, the two of them using a pair of frequent flyer tickets that I had accumulated from all my travels. That would leave me with fifteen-year-old Kelly, thirteen-year-old Sean, and nine-year-old Katie for ten days of togetherness in the mobile home that we had been living in for the past eight months. We had sold our house, and while deciding whether to buy or build, we had moved into a double-wide mobile home where living conditions were what might be called "snug."

"Well, at least there will be a little more room with Heather and me gone," Dottie offered.

"Yes, but I hope I can keep the place straightened up," I sighed. "I've got a big book deadline, and with the kids and all, I'm not sure I can handle everything the way I'd like."

"Oh, you'll do just fine," Dottie assured me. "And if it's a little messy when I get back, don't worry about it. I'm just so tickled to be able to go see my folks!"

While I was a little ambivalent about playing Mr. Mom for ten days, I still wanted Dottie to have the time away. I also wanted to seize the opportunity to reinforce our children's feelings of security by using the situation to remind them that their dad loved their mom very much. I wanted our kids to see how I was trying to apply the biblical principle, "Husbands, love your wives . . ." (Colossians 3:19). After I talked with Dottie about the trip, I sat down separately with each of the three older children and explained why Dottie was going to Florida.

"I love your mom very much, and while I know we're all going to miss her, I thought it was time that she took a break. She needs the rest and this chance to be with her family, and I just think one of the greatest ways I can show her how much I love her is to play Mr. Mom for a few days. It will be neat to have her go, but I'm going to need your help to make it work."

Kelly, Sean, and Katie nodded solemnly and committed themselves to help in every way they could. When I saw the "lists" Dottie prepared to remind me of everything that needed to be done, I was glad I'd gotten their commitment!

Mr. Mom Meets the "To-Do" List

"I usually just keep all this stuff in my head," Dottie told me cheerfully, as she handed me several sheets of paper on the way to the plane. "I thought maybe you could use a little help on keeping everything straight."

The first item on the list was getting everyone up at 6:30 to get ready for school. *That will be no problem,* I thought to myself, *I'll be getting up at 2:30 every morning to work on my book deadline anyway.*

But after that, things got a little more challenging. For example, there were the lunches: half a sandwich, some fruit, and a snack for each of the girls . . . full sandwich, extra fruit and two snacks for Sean . . . also, change to buy drinks. . . .

"I think I'll pack lunches the night before," I muttered to myself and went on to the rest of my assignment, which spelled out when each kid had to be at school. Because there were three different schools, there were three different times, but I figured we could handle that—after we got breakfast.

Yes, what about breakfast? One thing Mr. Mom doesn't do is cook very much, so it would be a bowl of cold cereal or we'd eat out. We ended up eating out most mornings at our favorite "dollar-and-something" place.

Once the kids were dropped off at school, I could go back home to work on my book, but then I had to be ready to pick them up that afternoon. Katie was a piece of cake because she wasn't involved in any sport at the time, and all I had to worry about was getting her to her 4-H sewing class on Wednesday. Kelly and Sean presented more of a challenge. They were both on basketball teams that practiced after school every day. In fact, Sean was on two teams and had to get to two different practice sessions in different parts of town.

Oh, yes, besides basketball practices, the kids had games— three for Sean and at least two for Kelly, as I recall. Most of them were played in Julian, but one of Sean's games was down in Ramona. We made them all and I got very familiar with the roads that ran up, down, and across the mountain.

I can see why Dottie sometimes calls herself a taxi driver, I mused as I went back and forth, picking up and delivering my kids and their friends. It all reminded me of a bumper sticker I had seen somewhere. How true it was: "If a Mother's Place Is in the Home, Why in the World Is She in the Car?"

And then there were dinners. To repeat, Mr. Mom doesn't cook, so it was either have Kelly or Sean cook or go out for dinner. We went out a few times. Once the kids made spaghetti (quite good, too), and on many nights we settled for microwave cuisine (which was also surprisingly tasty).

After dinner, there was homework—or getting the older children down to "Youth Alive," the church youth program. Sean went on Tuesday nights, Kelly on Wednesdays—more taxi service courtesy of Mr. Mom. Fortunately, the church was only a mile and a half away.

Bedtime provided its own special challenge. Naturally, every- one had his or her own particular approach to how long to stay up. Kelly, our night owl, was always last to go to bed and then often groped around groggily in the mornings. Sean, our lark, went to bed fairly early most nights and was up bright-eyed and bushy-tailed the next day. Katie was neither an owl nor a lark. She might go either way, depending on what she had been doing or what might be happening.

And Mr. Mom? Because I was on a deadline push and getting up to write every morning at 2:30, I was happy to head for bed with the chickens. But before I could go, I had to pack lunches for the next day, and also be sure everybody's outfit was laid out. I had always thought the kids just got themselves dressed, but my ten days as Mr. Mom taught me differently. There were certain kinds of outfits that went with certain kinds of other things. There were favorite this- and-thats, and, of course, certain colors went together while others didn't.

I had to be sure all this stuff was available and that meant doing the laundry. In fact, I did the laundry *several* times. As I poured generous amounts of "all-temperature" detergent into the machine, I wondered how in the world one family could use this much stuff in so short a time—and two of us weren't even there!

About halfway through my Mr. Mom stint, I suddenly realized how wise Dottie had been to take Heather with her.

"What would I do if I had a three-year-old to take care of, too?" I wondered aloud. I decided I didn't even want to think about it.

From the Routine to the Crisis

As the week wore on, the wheels started to come off the Mr. Mom Express just a little bit. One night I quickly got all the lunches together, put them in sacks, and congratulated myself on setting a new speed record. But the next morning as the girls looked in their sacks, I started hearing, "Where's my sandwich?"

Then Sean looked in his sack and said, "Wow! You sure gave me a lot to eat today!" It turned out I had put all the sandwiches in Sean's lunch!

After a few days, the kids started saying, "That's okay, Dad, I'll pack my own lunch." I wasn't sure how to take that. Were they trying to help or were they sending me a message? I thought I had been doing a pretty good job on lunches, but, as I heard someone say once, "You can con a con, you can fool a fool, but you can't kid a kid." From then on I let them pack their own lunches and everyone was happy—including me.

Not only did I get a taste of the hectic routine that Dottie experiences every time I'm away on a long trip, but I also got to go through one "special crisis" as well. It seems that the week I had picked to be Mr. Mom was also the week Sean had to get ready for entering his project in the annual Science Fair.

One day Sean handed me his list of all the materials, equipment, and supplies he needed for his project, most of which could be obtained only in San Diego, seventy miles away. There was only one thing to do. I made arrangements and pulled Sean out of school on Tuesday. We drove to San Diego, got all his stuff, and I got back in time to cover all my other bases as well.

But that wasn't all we had to do to get Sean prepared for the Science Fair. There were all kinds of reports and tests that had to be typed up. I admit I bailed out on that one and asked my secretary to help. I simply had no time because my book deadline was drawing nigh, and I had to keep working on that.

Somehow we got it all done and I breathed a sigh of relief. The Science Fair would be held the day after Dottie got back and I knew she wanted to go. I'd seen her handle other Science Fair preparations in prior years with ease, but as far as I was concerned, it had been a major ordeal. Mr. Mom was getting more insights on what it means to be a hero.

Mr. Mom Faces His Ultimate Challenge

As the day of Dottie's return approached, I realized there was good news and bad news. My wife would be back, and Mr. Mom would be relieved of some duties. But as I looked around the house, I saw the bad news. With all the running I had been doing with the kids and trying to keep the book manuscript going, the place had degenerated into what could only be called a disaster area.

I was in a tight spot. As I looked over my calendar, I saw that the book manuscript was due on Friday, and I also noted that I had scheduled a special weekend at the beach with the kids and some of their friends. The date had been set over a month before, and each of the children had been promised they could bring one or two friends along.

Now I always like to be a hero to my kids and their friends, but this time it was obvious I had picked the wrong weekend to do it. We'd be gone from Friday night to Sunday, and Dottie was due back Sunday evening. How could we get the place cleaned up in time?

Early Thursday morning I called all the children together for a conference: "We've got a problem here, gang. The house is a disaster and your mom's coming home on Sunday. I've got to work on my book manuscript, you've got to go to school, and Friday night we leave for your special weekend with your buddies at the beach. We can't back out on that, now can we?"

Three pairs of eyes told me that, indeed, we could not back out on the beach trip.

"Okay, it's obvious we can't have Mom come home to this mess. I love your mom very much and I know one of the greatest things we can do is leave this place absolutely immaculate. So, does anybody here have any friends whose mothers do cleaning? I know nothing could excite Mom more than coming home to a spick-and-span house."

I got a couple of vague references from the children, and, after dropping them off at school, I started making phone calls. Finally, somebody from our church told me about a lady who had just moved into the area. She did house cleaning and was supposed to be excellent. I called her and told her my problem.

"It sounds like it will take at least two days of work," she said. "If I provide the cleaning materials and supplies, it will be an additional $35.00."

"Lady, I wouldn't even know what to buy or how to start," I told her. "Throw in the supplies and I'll see you in the morning."

The woman arrived on Friday morning and I walked her through the house. She didn't seem too dismayed and set to work while I retreated to my office at The Julian Center to continue writing my book.

By late afternoon Friday I had finished the manuscript and I could see the cleaning lady had made some terrific headway. Floors and counters were starting to reappear from under the piles. I gave her the key to the house, picked up the kids, and we left for the beach trip.

When we got back on Sunday, I swung past the cleaning lady's home to find out how much I owed her. We hadn't set a price, and I had no idea of what cleaning services cost. I would soon get a crash course.

"I spent twenty-two hours over Friday and Saturday," she said. "With cleaning supplies, that comes to two hundred and fifty dollars."

I gulped and reached for my checkbook, rationalizing that Dottie had often spent many long hours reading, checking, and editing book manuscripts for me, and that this was a terrific opportunity to let her know how much I appreciated her.

As we pulled away, the kids noticed that I wasn't going back to our house, but I was heading for Dick and Charlotte Day's place.

"Why are we going this way," they wanted to know.

"Because you're staying at the Days' until Mom gets back. I'm not taking any chances on having you mess up the house."

"Aw, c'mon, Dad, we'll be careful. We'll just stay in the family room and probably use the bathroom a couple of times."

I shuddered. "Oh, no, you won't—I'd have you go out on the back hill first. I'm going to stash you at the Days' until Mom gets in."

I had already called Charlotte and had talked fast to convince her to take the kids for the afternoon and evening. It seemed she had problems of her own, and was trying to get her house ready for a big group that was coming over for a meeting at her place on Monday morning. As usual, Dick and Charlotte had understood and were willing to bail me out one more time.

I dropped the children off, thanked Dick and Charlotte fervently, and headed down to San Diego to pick up Dottie and Heather at the airport. I never was so glad to see anybody get off a plane in my life! As we drove back, Dottie told me how much she had appreciated her trip, and what a great time she had had with her family.

Then a little tentatively, she added, "Now, Josh, I know the house is probably a little messy, but don't you worry about it. I appreciate so much what you've done—being able to get away and see the folks has been super. So if there is a little cleaning to do, I understand."

Keeping a very straight face, I decided to play along: "Dottie, sweetheart, I'm afraid it is a bit messy. I tried my best, but I just couldn't get to it."

"Oh, that's all right, Josh," she reassured me. "It won't take long to straighten it up."

Dottie's words were brave, but as she told me later, she couldn't help but wonder. What could a not-too-neat writer-husband, two teen-agers, and a nine-year-old do to a double-wide mobile home in ten days? The Lord knew, but she could only guess.

We drove up to the house and when Dottie walked in and saw everything gleaming, neat and tidy, the first thirty seconds of her screams of surprise and "Oh, mys," were worth every bit of the two hundred and fifty dollars I had paid the cleaning lady. I even began thinking of an outline for a new book, "How to Be a Hero to Your Wife."

Suddenly it dawned on Dottie. "Where are the kids?" she wanted to know.

"Over at Dick and Charlotte's," I said with a grin. "I didn't want the place messed up before you got to see it."

We went over and picked up the kids and came back home. When fifteen-year-old Kelly, who hates to do housework and cleaning, saw the gleaming house, she made a comment that sort of put everything in context: "Wow! Dad, Mom is so lucky to be married to you!"

Kelly's compliment made me feel good, of course—it's always fun to be called a hero. But beyond that I was glad that Kelly had put the pieces together. I hadn't gotten the house cleaned at considerable expense because I was afraid of Dottie's wrath. I'd gotten it all cleaned up because I love her and I knew it was something that would please her very much. Once again, I'd struck another positive blow for my kids' security (not to mention my marriage).

Later I told Kelly, "I really appreciate what you said about Mom being lucky to be married to me, but I want you to know that I'm the one who's really lucky because I'm married to your mom and I have the privilege of being a dad to you kids."

Mr. Mom Learned a Lot about Relationships

That's my Mr. Mom story. Not exactly the stuff from which an episode of "Cosby" or "The Simpson's" might be made, but it was exciting enough for me, I assure you. And best of all, I learned some things about the challenges Dottie faces that I hadn't really understood before. I experienced "up close and personal" how hectic and frustrating her task can get at times.

And despite all the hassles with schedules and lunches, it was a great ten days with three of my children. I got to relate to them in just a little different context as Mr. Mom, and it all put new meaning in those words I often say: "Rules without relationships lead to rebellion."

There is something about grappling together with basic routines, schedules, and general demands of daily life that makes you aware of why a home needs rules and how important relationships are to keep it all going smoothly.

In the book of Proverbs, King Solomon said at one point:

My son, keep your father's commands and do not forsake your mother's teaching. Bind them upon your heart forever; fasten them around your neck. When you walk, they will guide you; when you sleep, they will watch over you; when you awake, they will speak to you. For the commands are a lamp, this teaching is a light, and the corrections of discipline are the way to life (Proverbs 6:20–23, NIV).

That's good advice. Solomon understood the need for rules and children obeying parents. Unfortunately, he came up short on relationships and had to pay the price. Solomon obviously had a lot of good intentions—his book of Proverbs is filled with them. But good intentions don't always become reality unless you keep working at it.

Remember, it's not the big things that count. It's the little things that you do day in and day out. Never give up. Every bit of what you do will be worth it. Never stop working at being a hero to your kids!

Appendix

The Hero's Tool Box

(More Ideas for What to Do with Your Children)

FOLLOWING is a collection of other activities and techniques we have used—and still use—to spend meaningful time with our kids while we make meaningful memories.

A special memory we made on an Easter Sunday was a trip to Laguna Beach, where we made sand castles—but not just any old kind of sand castle. Before we started, we read the entire Passion Week account from the Scriptures. All of us had parts and represented certain characters, and then we built the whole Passion Week scene in the sand—the cross, the tomb, the stone. We even made a "body" out of sticks tied together with seaweed. We had Golgotha with three crosses on the top—there was a lot of detail considering that all we had to work with was sand, some driftwood, and some bits of seaweed.

The kids never forgot it, and in fact we did it again a year or two later. Not only was it a great way to spend time together, but it was a great way for Dottie and me to teach our kids one of the most important parts of the Bible. Now that Heather is getting old enough to appreciate the Easter story, we plan to do the same thing again.

On another occasion I went out and bought a big magnifying glass and said to the kids, "Let's all go to the beach."

I might as well have said "Let's all go to Disneyland," or something like that because the kids love sand crabs and all the other creatures that inhabit the shoreline. We went down there and found all kinds of crabs, bugs, and other weird things.

It was about an hour and a half of sheer excitement with the kids, just jabbering, talking, and sharing. And at the same time I was able to relate it all to God's creation and talk about how He made every living creature unique. And then I said to them: "You know, son, you're unique. You know, girls, each of you is unique. God has made you different from everyone else."

And we did it all while peering through a magnifying glass I had bought at the local dime store. We had it on one bug so long I think we fried him, but it was a great time—another memory they won't ever forget.

In chapter 12, I mentioned some questions to ask your children to get them to share feelings and what they think. Here are some additional ideas: "When did you have the most fun? When was the time you felt the most embarrassed? When did you cry the hardest? When was the time when you were the most tired you've ever been in your life? Where were you when you were so tired?"

Two other good ones are: "When have you felt closest to God? When do you feel farthest away from God?"

Another question that's fun is, "If you invited Jesus to dinner tonight, what would you wear?" The first time that I asked this we were sitting at the dinner table and we went around and everybody said what he or she would wear. Then we talked about what we'd have to eat. It was interesting hearing the kids list their favorite dishes. Then I wondered who they would invite over to eat dinner with the Savior. Each of the children chose a non-Christian friend because he was sure that friend "would listen to Jesus."

Another exercise Dottie and I have done with the kids is "complete old sayings." Some of these include: "Don't put all your . . . Don't bite the hand . . . If at first you don't succeed . . ." And one of the best ones is, "Children should be seen and . . ."

After you've taken the family to the circus, as you're leaving ask, "Kids, what performance or performer did you see that best describes you and why?" Or go to the county fair and ask, "What kind of animal or display did you see today that best describes you and why?"

Another good one is, "If I could visit any place in the world I would go to . . ." and let them finish it. There are all kinds of completion statements like this. "If I had a million dollars, I would . . . If I could ask God one question, I'd ask Him . . . If I had a wishing rock, I would wish . . . If I were an Oscar Mayer wiener I would . . ."

Sometimes when I'm driving the kids to school I will say, "Tonight at the dinner table I want each of you to be able to share three things that you were thankful for today. Or share about three people you said thank you to today and why."

We do this now and then and our youngest child, Heather, will come up with one while our oldest child, Kelly, may come up with four or five. Dottie and I usually wind up with two or three.

My children have taught me that I can learn a lot in the rearview mirror. On one occasion, I phoned home while I was on a trip, and as Dottie and I were talking, I learned that Sean was due to take one of his projects to the Science Fair the next day.

"Do you think I could drive the kids down to the fair?" I asked Dottie.

"Well, I think they have all the drivers they need, but you never know."

After hanging up with Dottie, I called Sean's teacher and asked her if I could take a van load of kids to the Science Fair. It turned out they didn't have enough drivers and she was delighted. When I got home the next night from my trip, I was beat, but I had made a commitment. I went in and woke Sean up at midnight and asked him what was happening tomorrow.

"We're gonna take projects down to the Science Fair," he said sleepily.

"Would you like to have me drive?" I asked my son, wondering where I'd get the strength to get up early the next morning and drive a van full of kids all the way to San Diego.

"Would you, Dad?"

"I've already talked to your teacher, and I'm scheduled," I told Sean with a big smile.

"Wow! Are you going to bring the ice chest?"

"We'll see," I said with a wink.

The next morning I wound up with Sean and five other kids in the van, plus one other special item that made me a hero, indeed. It was an ice chest filled with candy bars, New York Seltzers, and other favorite goodies.

"Hey," Sean exclaimed to his friends. "Look at what my dad got us! This is gnarly! You're the coolest, Dad!"

Now, I realize some moms in particular might not think it's good to feed kids candy, but I justify it for a couple of reasons. It's the only time I ever make that much candy available, and while my kids are snacking and talking in the back seat I accomplish my real mission—watching the rearview mirror and listening to what goes on. What I'm really out to do is learn how Sean is adjusting. How is he doing relationally with his friends? What do they talk about and how do they get along?

Is Sean ever arrogant? Is he timid? Does he share?

I learn more about my kids and how they relate to others by driving them places than in any other way. Once I took Kelly and her friends to a Lakers game, and afterward we stopped at a restaurant for a sundae. Even when I'm talking to one of the kids, I'm listening to everything. I pick up all kinds of things—good and bad.

On one trip, I heard one of Sean's friends saying to Sean from the back of the van, "Go ahead and tell him you did it." I quickly saw that Sean's friend was encouraging him to lie about something—a chore or other duty he hadn't done before we left perhaps. When we stopped at a gas station I took the boy aside and confronted him gently but firmly: "I really didn't appreciate what I heard you tell Sean a few miles back."

In that situation, the boy responded well. He apologized and as a result of our little chat he "shaped up." In other cases, the response has not always been so positive, and Dottie and I have encouraged Sean to cool the relationship with that particular person. I know that for a lot of parents, making comments to your children's friends can be venturing in where angels fear to tread. Yet that is what I want other parents to do with my kids. And so far, I've been lucky, and I believe a lot of it is that I've made my own luck by being a dad who does fun stuff and provides special things on trips down the mountain.

You might say that being a hero to Sean and his friends gives me a "right" to be heard. Then my opinion about who makes a good friend and who doesn't carries some weight with my son—or my daughter, as the case may be.

A key principle to being a hero to your kids and their friends is to focus on *their world,* not yours. I remember talking to one dad who said, "I offered to take my kid out to have a good time, but he didn't have any fun at all—the whole thing was a big failure."

"What did you do with him?" I wondered.

"Well, I love to golf, so I took him golfing," the dad said insistently. "It turns out he hates golfing, so I guess that's that."

This incident really happened—I'm not making it up! This father wanted to spend time with his boy, but on *his* terms and at *his* convenience. I had to let him know that he was a bit unclear on the concept. He had to focus in on his boy's world and do what *he* wanted if he hoped to build any kind of relationship with his son.

Focusing on their world can take time—and it can be a lot of bother—but it can also be a lot of fun. I'm always asking myself, "What is Sean into now? What is Kelly interested in during this particular year in school? What is Katie like? And what about little Heather—what is her world all about right now?

I can remember when Sean was a little guy and he was into Superman. In fact, he had a Superman cape that he wore everywhere. Talk about Linus and his blanket! If we needed to discipline Sean, all we had to do is take away his cape. It was like cutting Samson's hair. Life simply wasn't worth living for him without that Superman cape!

So with all this competition from Superman, I decided to read up on him. I bought a big pile of Superman comic books and pretty soon I knew as much about Superman as Sean did. I also gave Sean the comics, which he dearly treasured. His Superman stage didn't last long, but while it did, I did my best to play Clark Kent and it paid off.

A few years later, when Sean was around ten, his big interest was sports cars. And I mean the expensive ones—the Mazzerattis, the Lamborghinis, and the Ferrari Testerozas. As I saw Sean finding pictures of these cars in magazines and newspaper ads, I could see his interest was more than casual, and I got an idea.

I got out the Yellow Pages and picked out some of the top sports car agencies in Beverly Hills. Then I sent each car dealer a letter that said:

I'm a desperate dad. I'll do anything to spend time with my son, and right now he's into sports cars. Would it be possible if I pulled him out of school and brought him up to your showroom so that we could take some test drives? I want to tell you up front, I'm not interested in buying a car.

Amazingly, I got positive replies from every dealer. I called and made appointments for us and we drove up to Beverly Hills (a distance of some one hundred and fifty miles) for a day in the sports car showrooms. And what a day it was. Sean went out alone on "test drives" with salesmen and "tried out" just about every big name car you can think of. As they came by the showroom, Sean would wave to me—he was so proud.

And along with the test drives, he got posters, some of which were autographed by famous race car drivers. All in all, it was an incredible day, and on the way home we discussed which cars we liked the best and went over all the flyers, books, and posters he had collected. Then I gently switched the subject and started talking to Sean about looking at all this in the light of the Great Commission.

"You know, Sean, all these cars are fun, but they cost huge amounts of money. What we should be thinking about is what God has called us to as a family. . . ." And with that beginning I was able to communicate to Sean one of the best lessons on materialism I could have ever possibly taught. I didn't make it preachy, but I did make my point about things and how we may like certain things and enjoy them, but their cost puts them in another category compared to where we are as Christians and servants of Christ.

Sean understood. He knew I wasn't asking him to throw out his posters or his flyers. He knew I didn't mind if he still liked to look at the sports cars, but he also knew a little more about materialism—and values—before we got home.

Three months later, that was the end of the sports cars. Sean was on to other things. You may wonder, "Was it worth it—all that time and trouble?" I think it was, and so do at least ten other dads who've told me they've done the same thing after hearing me tell about it at seminars.

The point is, the sports car trip is one illustration of stepping into your child's world. When you can do that with full acceptance of his world and of him, then you earn the right to be heard about your own values and convictions.

Just recently, ten-year-old Katie has taken a real interest in baseball. She watched a lot of the playoff games with Dottie, who is a die-hard Boston Red Sox fan who grew up in the Boston area. I plan to get a complete set of baseball cards to present to Katie as a gift, saying, "I'll work on baseball cards with you. I'll try to get signatures of some of the star players when I speak to their teams."

Katie, of course, will be thrilled. This will be our new project, something we'll do as long as she is interested. I'm kind of looking forward to it. (And I hope I can make good on my promise to get Jose Canseco's autograph during the World Series!)

Over the years I've made it a goal with my older children to spend time discussing national and international events and their meaning. I try to pick up on things to which I can apply a moral or a value—something to live by.

Recently, while on a trip when the children were along, I took several hours in our motel room to talk to them about what had happened in the Middle East when Iraq invaded Kuwait. I went into the history of the region, what had motivated Saddam Hussein to do what he did, and some of the biblical background on the history of the Arabs and Jews. It was a great opportunity to teach the children about hatred and how it can poison people over many centuries of time. It was also a great opportunity to talk about the need for forgiveness.

The headlines and television newscasts are full of opportunities to "seize the teachable moment" to have worthwhile discussions with your children. A few years ago, while visiting Germany, then-President Ronald Reagan paid a visit to a cemetery in Bitburg, where about one hundred Nazi soldiers are buried. As he placed a wreath at the tomb of the German equivalent of the Unknown Soldier, President Reagan said: "It is time to put the war behind us. It's time to forgive."

Reagan's actions and comment caused a furor back in the U.S. Polls showed over fifty percent of the citizens were against him, and some senators and congressmen even called for his impeachment.

Although approximately forty years had elapsed since World War II, people said that it had not been enough time. It wasn't time to forgive because the world might forget and then the same thing might happen again.

Along with my children, I watched all of the television newscasts reporting what had happened. I read them articles from the paper about Bitburg, and finally I said, "Kids, let's go out and have breakfast and talk about what Mr. Reagan has said and what it means."

Kelly, Sean, and I went down to the Julian Cafe and there in a packed restaurant, where almost everybody in the room knew me and my children (Julian is a very small town), we discussed President Reagan's visit to Bitburg in light of Matthew 6:12, part of the Lord's Prayer: "Forgive us our debts, as we also have forgiven our debtors" (NIV).

As I was pointing out that what President Reagan had done was simply tell the entire nation that it was time to forgive, one of the waitresses overheard me, and in front of the packed restaurant, at the top of her voice, she let me have it with both barrels.

"Mr. McDowell, Reagan is an evil man and so are you for teaching this stuff to your children."

If the waitress had said, "My broker is E. F. Hutton," she couldn't have gotten more attention. The place stopped dead and everyone stared. She stomped back toward the counter and halfway across the room she wheeled around, pointed her finger at me and snapped, "And I can tell you something else, Mr. McDowell. If President Reagan's mother had been gassed by the Nazis, he never would have gone to Bitburg!"

My kids were all eyes. I thought to myself, *What an opportunity!*

"Kids, what do you think about what the lady just said?" I said loudly enough for the rest of the room to hear. Kelly, my oldest piped up, "Daddy, that's one person's opinion!"

"No, what do you really think?" I persisted. "If President Reagan's mother had been killed by the Nazis, would he have gone to Bitburg? That's really not the right question, is it?"

By now everyone in the restaurant was wondering, *What* is *the right question?*

"The right question is," I continued, "if his mother had been killed by the Nazis, *should* he have gone to Bitburg?"

And then I was able to go on to make the point that all of the people who had damned President Reagan for his plea for forgiveness were really saying, "God, don't forgive us, because we are not willing to forgive the Nazis."

You may not want to get into debates with waitresses in restaurants over international issues in front of your children, but you can pick your own time and place to talk about some of these things. Ask them for their opinions and then quietly give them yours.

Instead of investing in things, try investing in experiences. One of the greatest examples of this I know of was Dick and Charlotte Day taking Jonathan and Timmy, their two younger sons, on a special tour of Europe when the boys were fourteen and fifteen years old. They traveled for five weeks by Eurorail pass, backpacks on their backs, staying in youth hostels or little fourth-floor walk-up pensions, where they all had to live in one room together. Not only did the trip give the boys an opportunity to see different cultures, but it also helped give them a greater sense of world history as well as present-day events.

Dick calls that trip a phenomenal investment. At the time the family really needed a car, but he and Charlotte have never regretted investing in something far more important.

You may not be able to take your children to Europe, but figure out a special trip you could take that has a specific theme or purpose. The point is, *invest in an experience together.* The dividends it can pay are inestimable.

Right along with the idea of taking a special trip together, think about taking your children along on your next business trip, if this is at all possible. I do this quite often, and one thing I've learned is to plan ahead so I can keep my child busy.

I usually only invite one child at a time to accompany me when I'm on a speaking tour. I will phone ahead and have people in churches where I am speaking arrange activities for my son or daughter while I'm busy working. Then, when I am not speaking or conducting meetings, I can spend plenty of one-on-one time with the child as well.

On one occasion when Sean was with me, I learned that a family in a church where I would be speaking had another boy Sean's age who was deeply involved in skateboarding. The town where we were visiting had a special skateboard park, and the boy's parents were happy to have Sean go along with their son to try all the ramps and chutes. For two days, Sean had the time of his life.

On another trip, Katie flew in to meet me on the last day of a speaking engagement. Again, with help of people in the church where I was speaking, I was able to arrange some special activities for her.

The point is, my kids love to travel with me on the road, not because they are crazy about watching me work, but because I arrange "fun stuff" for them to do while I am working. Then, when I'm not working, we really enjoy our times together.

Mealtimes are great for doing things with your children, especially if you have teen-agers, who never seem to be around at family meals. But a special meal could be a great drawing card. Have you ever tried having dinner or lunch in the bedroom, or maybe in your garage? Your kids will never forget it. Another thing you can do is play "switch-a-roo." I will take one of the children aside in the morning and tell them, "Tonight at dinner you are in charge. You sit in my chair and whatever you say goes for what we eat and do."

Then I have them work things out with Dottie and we allow the child who's playing "Dad" for the evening to decide on the menu. This had led to some very interesting meals, including ice cream for appetizers and peanut butter and jelly sandwiches for the main course. Don't do this unless you're ready for just about anything, but if you decide to do it, it will make a tremendous hit with your kids, I assure you. It's a different way to tell each one, "You are special."

Another great way to turn mealtime into unforgettable chaos is to have a "progressive fast food dinner." Go to different fast food restaurants for different courses, letting your children choose the menu. That might mean Taco Bell for a tostada salad, the local pizza shop for the main course, and McDonald's for apple turnovers for dessert. Warning: Do not try this unless you have a strong stomach or a good supply of Tums!

Endnotes

Chapter 1

1. "Where's Dad?" *Washington Watch,* published by Family Research Council, January, 1990, p. 2. Quoted in *The Josh McDowell Research Almanac and Statistical Digest,* p. 1101.
2. "Day Care Cities-Problem," *USA Today,* August 29, 1989. Quoted in *The Josh McDowell Research and Statistical Digest,* p. 99.
3. Jean L. Richardson, et al., "Substance Abuse among Eighth Grade Students Who Take Care of Themselves after School," *Pediatrics,* 1989, pp. 556–565. Quoted in *The Josh McDowell Research and Statistical Digest,* p. 110.
4. *Fundamentalist Journal,* October 1984. Quoted in *The Josh McDowell Research and Statistical Digest,* p. 86.
5. "Focus on the Family Bulletin," 1989. Quoted in *The Josh McDowell Research and Statistical Digest,* p. 87.
6. "Report to the President: White House Conference on Children." Washington D.C., U.S. Government Printing Office, 1971, pp. 41–43.
7. Robert Hemfelt, Frank Minirth, Paul Meier, *Love Is a Choice* (Nashville: Thomas Nelson Publishers, 1989), see p. 12.
8. Ibid., p. 11.
9. Ibid., p. 14.
10. Adapted from the poem, "Children Learn What They Live," by Dorothy Law Nolte. This poem is often published under "author unknown" and appears to be in public domain.
11. For these thoughts about "What Is A Hero?" I am indebted to a poem attributed to Jimmy Stewart, which he quoted during a "Hope for a Drug-Free America" program as part of Super Bowl activities. His poem is quoted by Doris Lee McCoy, in her book *Megatraits: Twelve Traits of Successful People* (Plano, Texas: Wordware Publishing Inc., 1988).
12. Robert S. McGee, Jim Craddock, Pat Springle, *The Parent Factor* (Houston: Rapha Publishing, 1989), p. 9.
13. "Children Learn What They Live," by Dorothy Law Nolte.

Chapter 2

1. Josh McDowell, *How to Help Your Child Say No to Sexual Pressure,* (Waco: Word Books Publisher, 1987), p. 51.
2. Statistics from *Junior High Ministry,* May-August, 1988. Quoted in *The Josh McDowell Research and Statistical Digest,* p. 104.

Chapter 4

1. Josh McDowell, *Building Your Self-Image* (Wheaton: Living Books, Paperback Edition, 1988), p. 25.

Chapter 5

1. Charles Caldwell Ryrie, Editor, *Ryrie Study Bible* (Chicago: Moody Press, 1976), p. 968.
2. For a full discussion of the "eight ages of man," see Erik H. Erikson, *Childhood and Society,* Second Edition revised and enlarged (New York: W. W. Norton and Company, Inc., 1964), pp. 247–273.
3. "I Am Loved." Words by William J. & Gloria Gaither. Music by William J. Gaither. © Copyright 1978 by William J. Gaither. All rights reserved. International copyright secured. Used by permission.

Chapter 6

1. Dr. James Dobson, *Hide or Seek* (Old Tappan: Fleming H. Revell Company, 1974), see pp. 23ff.
2. See Stephen D. Eyre, *Defeating the Dragons of the World* (Downers Grove: InterVarsity Christian Fellowship, 1987), p. 24.
3. Ibid.

Chapter 7

1. Kenneth Blanchard, Spencer Johnson, *The One-Minute Manager* (New York: Berkeley Books, 1983).

Chapter 8

1. For an excellent discussion of the characteristics of a perfectionist, see David Stoop, *Living With a Perfectionist* (Nashville: Oliver Nelson, 1987).
2. Roger Maris' record sixty-one home runs was accomplished during a schedule considerably longer than the one in which Ruth hit his sixty.
3. Erikson, *Childhood and Society,* pp. 258–261.

Chapter 9

1. See McDowell, *How to Help Your Child Say "No" to Sexual Pressure,* p. 28.

2.   "Condoms Sought in School," San Diego Union, Thursday, March 15, 1990, p. C–4. Quoted in *The Josh McDowell Research and Statistical Digest,* p. 1.

3.   Josh McDowell, Dick Day, *Why Wait?* (San Bernardino: Here's Life Publishers, Inc., 1987). For a total report on the reasons why youth have premarital sex, see Part 2, pp. 71–185.

4.   "Summary of Findings: Young Adolescents and Their Parents." Search Institute, Minneapolis, MN, 1984, p. 1D.

5.   H. Norman Wright, *Always Daddy's Girl* (Ventura: Regal Books, 1989), p. 10.

6.   See Erikson, *Childhood and Society,* pp. 261–263.

7.   See Erikson, *Childhood and Society,* pp. 263–266.

8.   Debora Phillips, *Sexual Confidence* (Boston: Houghton Mifflin, 1980), p. 121.

Chapter 10

1.   Rolf Garborg, *The Family Blessing* (Dallas: Word Publishing, 1990).

Chapter 11

1.   See Josh McDowell, *How to Help Your Child Say "No" to Sexual Pressure,* p. 19.

2.   Anthony Casale, *Tracking Tomorrow's Friends* (Kansas City: Andrews, Mcmeel and Parker, 1986). This publication was a book compiled by the Ganett New Media Services, *USA Today,* and featured compilation of research and polls taken by *USA Today* on various subjects and issues. The publication is no longer in print.

Chapter 14

1.   See Jennifer Warren, "Malnourished Girl Found Locked in Closet; Parents Held," *The Los Angeles Times,* Thursday, October 25, 1990, p. A3.

2.   See Dr. James Dobson, *Dare to Discipline* (Wheaton: Tyndale House Publishers, 1970), Introduction page 1–4.

LET'S STAY -IN- TOUCH!

If you have grown personally as a result of this material, we should stay in touch. You will want to continue in your Christian growth, and to help your faith become even stronger, our team is constantly developing new materials.

We are now publishing a monthly newsletter called 5 Minutes with Josh which will

1) tell you about those new materials as they become available
2) answer your tough questions
3) give creative tips on being an effective parent
4) let you know our ministry needs
5) keep you up to date on my speaking schedule (so you can pray).

If you would like to receive this publication, simply fill out the coupon below and send it in. By special arrangement 5 Minutes with Josh will come to you regularly — no charge.

Let's keep in touch!

Josh

☐ **Yes!** I want to receive the free subscription to **5 Minutes with JOSH**

_____
NAME

_____
ADDRESS

_____
CITY, STATE/ZIP

SLC-2024

Mail To:
Josh McDowell
c/o 5 Minutes with Josh
Campus Crusade for Christ
Arrowhead Springs
San Bernardino, CA 92414

Additional Resources by Josh McDowell

Books

The Teenage Q&A Book (Josh McDowell and Bill Jones)
Friend of the Lonely Heart (Josh McDowell and Norm Wakefield)
How to Help Your Child Say "No" to Sexual Pressure
It Can Happen to You
Unlocking the Secrets of Being Loved, Accepted, and Secure (Josh McDowell and Dale Bellis)
Love, Dad

Video

How to Be a Hero to Your Kids (Josh McDowell and Dick Day)
It Can Happen to You
Friend of the Lonely Heart (Josh McDowell and Norm Wakefield)
WHY WAIT? Video Collection:
      Why Waiting Is Worth the Wait
      God Is No Cosmic Kill-joy
      How to Handle the Pressure Lines
      A Clean Heart for a New Start
Evidence for Faith Series
How to Help Your Child Say "No" to Sexual Pressure
Let's Talk about Love and Sex
The Myths of Sex Education
"No!"—The Positive Answer
Where Youth Are Today
Who Do You Listen To?

Audio

How to Be a Hero to Your Kids (Josh McDowell and Dick Day)
Friend of the Lonely Heart (Josh McDowell and Norm Wakefield)
The Teenage Q&A Book on Tape
Why Wait? What You Need to Know about the Teen Sexuality Crisis (Josh
    McDowell and Dick Day)
How to Help Your Child Say "No" to Sexual Pressure
"No!"—The Positive Answer (Love Waiting music)
The Secret of Loving
Why Waiting Is Worth the Wait

16 mm Films

Evidence for Faith Series
Messianic Prophecy
Misconceptions about Christianity, Part I
Misconceptions about Christianity, Part II
The Reliability of Scripture
A Skeptic's Quest
The Uniqueness of the Bible
Where Youth Are Today: What You Need to Know about the Teen Sexuality
    Crisis

Available from your Christian bookstore or Word Publishing

HOW TO BE A HERO TO YOUR KIDS

BY JOSH McDOWELL AND DICK DAY

Now that you have just completed *How To Be A Hero To Your Kids*, you can share what you've learned with others through the *How To Be A Hero To Your Kids* video. Josh McDowell and Dick Day share practical suggestions for positive parenting and teach moms and dads how to put these principles to work.

How To Be A Hero To Your Kids video cassette comes with a leader's guide, reproducible discussion guide and a copy of the *How To Be A Hero To Your Kids* book. It's perfect for group study and a must for all parents.

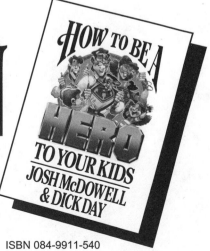

ISBN 084-9911-540